Boss Women Rock:

How to Go from Best Kept Secret to Sought After Expert

Jen DeVore Richter

Disclaimer

Dedication

With God all things are possible.

The best gift He ever gave me is my loving husband Will Richter who has been with me through the trials, tribulations and triumphs of being an entrepreneur. He doesn't just support me from afar either, he's flown with me to keynote speeches out of state, sold my books from the back of the room, and is the first person I go to with my ideas. He's my rock.

To the women of the Boss Women Rock community and to those of you who contributed to this book... your trust and belief in me is humbling. Your drive and determination to succeed is inspiring. Your willingness to serve others is admirable. This book is for you.

To the reader of this book, I hope you will take the concepts presented in this book and use them for good. Use them to shine a light on the people, causes, and missions that you care about. God gave you gifts and talents and He wants you to use them to help other people overcome their challenges. Start now...

Why you should read this book:

This book is for you if you are a coach, consultant, or service based professional that has a message to spread. If what you do can change someone's life by helping them get healthy, save money in their personal life, make money in their business, protect their family, save their marriage, improve their relationship with their self, or just thrive in life if they only knew what you know, then this book will benefit you greatly.

Join the Boss Women Rock community and get access to bonus trainings, resources, and support from amazing people. Join us on Facebook at https:// www.facebook.com/groups/BossWomenRockSuccess

Boss Women Rock: How to Go from Best Kept Secret to Sought After Expert

Contents

Preface

How this book will transform your thinking about the importance of marketing your best ideas and information.

W*hat does it mean to go from best kept secret to sought after expert?*

Forget the tired concept of chasing after clients one at a time only to face rejection after rejection–there is no need to keep doing what doesn't work especially when the alternative is so much more fun and lucrative.

Whether your dream is to build a successful consulting business, grow your practice, or sell more services, *Boss Women Rock: How to Go from Best Kept Secret to Sought After Expert* has the blueprint.

This step-by-step guide to becoming a sought after expert teaches:

- How to start even if you don't have a big social media following, email list, or best selling book.

- How to avoid imposter syndrome and the other BS false lies that will try to hold you back from shining your light.

- How to share your story in a way that is relatable, exciting, and moves people to action without feeling braggadocious.

- How to connect with an audience that will actually care about your message and buy your business' products and services.

- How to build your primary business offer for maximum profitability and impact while getting paid your worth.

- Why direct response conversion and sales tactics prevents your marketing from just being a big waste of time and money.

- How to leverage small stages and events for maximum income, impact, and influence when the big meeting planners won't let you play in their sandbox.

- Which systems and resources make this process a ton more fun and a whole lot easier without breaking the bank.

My goal with this book is to shed light on the exact process I used to build the business of my dreams, so that you can too.

To your success!
Jen DeVore Richter

Chapter One

Knowing where to start even if you don't have a big social media following, email list, or best selling book.

W hat if everything you've ever heard about marketing is wrong? What would that change about the way you market your business?

My goal with writing this book is to finally shed light on the truth about what really works in small business marketing for experts and what is just a bunch of fluff-filled platitudes and misinformation handed down by well-meaning, but misinformed marketing gurus.

The reason why I wanted to write this book is because I see so many business owners struggling to launch or grow a business based on their expertise. When we get hit with the entrepreneurial bug it's like cupid's bow piercing right through our heart. We see a need in the market that we want to fill or we overcome a problem and want to help other people overcome that problem too by sharing our stories and transformational processes. Those are both great reasons for starting a business, but there has to be more. There has to be profit because your message is powered by profit.

Because your message is powered by profit.™

As an entrepreneur, it can be easy to get emotionally connected and invested to our businesses, sometimes to our own detriment. I have heard over and over again, "I love what I do so much, that I would do it for free." Well, guess what, with that attitude, you just might get to do it for free and your business will fail. I don't say that to be mean, but I do say it as a form of tough love. You need a proven process to follow to maximize profitability so that your message can be heard.

If you picked up this book looking for a motivational pep talk, a short-cut, or a shiny object, you're in the wrong place. If you picked up this book because you need a real deal, honest strategy and mindset shift on how to stand out then you're in the right place. I congratulate you for deciding to make a change starting today!

That is the first step toward becoming a Boss Woman who Rocks!

In this book, I am going to share with you the truth about how to grow a business so you can go from underpaid best kept secret to profitable sought after expert. Here is where you start.

Gains from reading Chapter One: Knowing where to start even if you don't have a big social media following, email list, or best selling book.

- How to stand out in a crowded and competitive marketplace without spending a fortune and wasting months or even years on tactics that don't work

- How to become seen as the go-to expert by making it about them, not about you

- How to generate leads instantly by changing one simple thing: what you say

Rumors and Reality:

- You may be thinking that becoming a sought after expert is not possible for you because you can't afford the time or money it takes to build a huge social media following, email list, or fancy photo shoot that makes you look like a supermodel, but the truth is that you don't need to spend gobs of money to move into the spotlight.

- You may be thinking that your industry is different and these strategies won't work because "this is just how it's always been done", but the truth is that these strategies work for ANY business in ANY industry, but they work especially well for coaches, consultants, and service based business owners.

- You may be thinking that you've heard it all before and this is just another fly-by-night shiny object, but the truth is that what I am about to share with you will because this is a proven step-by-step SYSTEM that works. At Boss Women Rock, we call it the Rising Influencer Profit Process™.

If you want elevate your visibility, increase your income, generate leads predictably, and gain control of your cash flow and business, then this is the most important thing you'll read all year.

Here's why...

The small business failure rate is on the rise leaving many with unfulfilled hopes and dreams of impacting the lives of others in a positive way. Business owners are feeling overwhelmed, frustrated, and burnt out from chasing 'shiny objects' in their business and listening to so-called 'marketing gurus' spout the next tip, trick or tactic only to get NO results.

According to the SBA, 80% of businesses FAIL in the first 18 months and if you make it to year 5, your chance of failure is 50%. But you don't have to fail!

I'm here to shed light on the truth about how to build a profitable expert business you love leveraging your unique gifts and talents.
In fact, you will become a magnet and attract the ideal, perfect clients that you want to help while improving profitability from the start.

In this chapter, we're examining:

Generating All the Leads Your Business Can Handle:

So, here's the big secret no one talks about when it comes to generating leads and being seen as the go-to expert:

It's not about you.

Yep, building a personal brand and business is not about talking about yourself incessantly, taking selfies, and raving on about how great you are. No one cares about your degrees, diplomas, how many years you've been in business, and all the other self-serving platitudes we see every day.

Building a personal brand and becoming a sought after expert in your industry is about *them*. It's about the people you serve, the mission you are on, and the problem you solve.

To begin, ask "who" instead of "what."

> *The #1 secret to marketing success: have something good to say, say it well, say it often. To do this, get inside the heart and mind of your ideal, perfect client and understand their problems.*

Yesterday, I received a phone call from a brand new business coach. This coach was struggling to generate leads for her business because she was doing what most people do when they start a business. She printed up some business cards, joined the Chamber of Commerce and headed to a networking event. Guess what happened at the networking event? Nothing that would drive her business forward.

She met some nice people, sat through about 30 self-centered elevator pitches, and at the end of the event, one sales person came up to her and asked for her business card so they could "buy her a coffee to pick her brain" (hint: try to sell her something.) Her competition was in the room, and she received zero real leads. What a big waste of time!

I asked her to give the 30 second pitch she used at the event. This is what she said:

"Hi, my name is Susan. I am a business coach who has 5 years of experience. My goal is to build my business here in Jacksonville because I really love this area and am passionate about everything I do. If you need a website design, or social media management, or brochure done, or need help with your business. Let me know. Thanks."

So, the first thing that I see wrong with this approach is that it's all about what Susan wants, it's too broad, and has no call to action. There is nothing unique or special about it that would make people think that she is an expert.

I gave her an example alternative approach using my own networking pitch as an example:

"Have you spent thousands of dollars on marketing only for it to have NO impact on your bottom line? Are you frustrated and overwhelmed by marketing? My name is Jen DeVore and I am a Business Breakthrough Specialist. I work with coaches, consultants and service based professionals who are experts in their industries, but frustrated from lack of profit. I deliver breakthroughs, fast and in little as 45 minutes.

I've started a movement for women in business called Boss Women Rock to inspire and empower them to build a profitable business following my proven system.

I have the unique ability to find any business owner $10,000 in hidden revenue opportunities just by taking a look at your existing marketing. I can do this process in 45 minutes. I call it my $10K Challenge. Put me to the test in your business! Come see me after the meeting to pick up a free copy of my latest book where I detail the process for you."

Do you see the difference in the two elevator pitches?

The first (Susan's) is about her. It's generic, and it's boring.

The second (mine) is about the pain business owners suffer, it's about them and what they want (to make money and get a breakthrough fast), it introduces a proven process (my $10K Challenge), and it has a special, informational offer that positions me as an authority (the book.)

What business owners need is to make and save money. They need a proven process to follow. They need an expert. By changing her messaging, Susan could dominate her marketplace and make her competition irrelevant.

To become a sought after expert, you need to say things differently. Doing and saying things differently will move you into the spotlight and have people clamor to work with you. Be the rebel in your industry and specific on who you serve.

> *Become relevant and important to*
> *ONE type of client.*

Most people start their day by watching the news, but what if you were able to be the person that was making the news? I saw this question posed by a friend on Facebook today and it got me thinking...

Most coaches, consultants, and service professionals that are trying to build an expert business and move into the spotlight don't realize how easy it is to become newsworthy and they struggle to get attention for their business.

But, when you become relevant growing your business becomes easy. When you are the person that's in the spotlight you can take that spotlight and shine it on whatever you want.

You can take the attention and shine it on your business, a service, a special event, or a cause you support because you're the person that's controlling the conversation. You're setting the tone for what people are talking about.

It helps you save on advertising. It helps you strengthen your relationships in your community. It gives you instant authority so that you can achieve success faster.

What's my secret to becoming newsworthy? Basically: have something interesting to say. Don't make it all about you. Tell a story that inspires others and encourages them to become a better version of themselves.

Clients, event organizers, journalists, TV producers, podcast hosts and people that are in the media do not consider information about your company to be newsworthy.

They're looking for how you impact the community. They're looking for what difference you make to their listeners, readers, or viewers or themselves.

Write your answers below:

How does what you do impact the lives of others? Think in terms of improving someone's health, wealth, or relationships.

What problem do your potential clients have that you can solve and potentially change their life?

What pleasure do they want, but don't have that you can help them obtain?

Boss Women Rock: It works!

Ana Stauch
2 reviews

★ ★ ★ ★ ★ a week ago

"Jen, before hiring you I felt like I had lost control over the money in my business. I didn't really know what I should and should not do to grow. Now I am in complete control and actually enjoying the process. Plus, we're measuring our results everyday. Putting profit first and focusing on pricing has enabled us to generate more cash flow faster. It's only been a couple days and I see the difference financially! Plus, the strategies you created for me to generate leads are going to be really fun."

April Caldwell
5 reviews

★ ★ ★ ★ ★ 4 months ago

Working with Jen was such a fun and productive experience. We got an amazing amount of work done, put processes to my business and I left with such motivation to go and implement what we talked about. Within 24 hours I made back my investment by signing a high ticket client.

Zelda Greenberg
2 reviews

★ ★ ★ ★ ★ 4 months ago

Jen is the real deal! I've wasted thousands of dollars on gurus, coaches, & consultants... all a waste of money and time. I met Jen and in 2 days I learned more about how to market my business than all those other experts combined. She helped me figure out how to put together a clear plan to move my business forward quickly and in the most cost effective way. Jen is by far the best investment of time and money to move your business UP...(i.e. more money and more clients). Hire Jen!

Results Wrap Up:

Iif you had a process to follow that would empower you to craft a market dominating position statement and messaging that was client focused, do you think you could be successful?

Yes! You can. To get started, you just need to take the Next Step Action.

Take Action:

- Your action assignment for this chapter is to rewrite your market dominating position statement. Begin by getting inside the mind of your ideal, perfect client and think about what problems they have that you can solve. How can you do it better, different, faster, cheaper, or at a better level of quality? Remember, the bigger the problem you solve, the bigger your paycheck, so make it a good one.

- If you don't know what problems your clients have, ask them what keeps them up at night. What is the conversation they are having around the kitchen table with their spouse that they need to solve? What do they not like about your industry that you could change and turn into your competitive advantage?

- Alternatively, what pleasure do they want that they don't have? How would it feel to them to lose the weight, build their business, save their marriage, buy the house? Write down the words they use to describe it and how you can build a business to give them the result.

Join the Boss Women Rock community and get access to bonus trainings, resources, and support from amazing people. Join us on Facebook at https:// www.facebook.com/groups/BossWomenRockSuccess

Chapter Two

Avoiding imposter syndrome and the other BS false lies that will try to hold you back from stepping into the spotlight.

I often hear from potential clients that they don't want to talk about themselves or they are afraid of selling themselves so they remain in the shadows. This is especially true of those that are new to an industry.

Imposter Syndrome is a psychological pattern in which an individual doubts their accomplishments and has a persistent internalized fear of being exposed as a fraud.

Basically, it means that although you are capable and qualified to be seen as an expert, you will sabotage yourself with self-doubt, worry, and shrink back instead of step forward.

If you are in a highly regulated industry with lots of "traditional" ways of doing things this may come up especially for you. I see this predominantly in highly regulated industries like legal, medicine and finance.

If you have ever had feelings of self doubt and aren't sure that you will be accepted as an "expert" this section is for you.

If you have ever felt jealous or envious of someone else in your industry who is further ahead in building their business or brand, then this chapter is for you.

Or if you have ever laid in bed at night rethinking your plan and doubting if you really have what it takes to market yourself as an expert, this chapter is for you.

Gains from Reading Chapter Two: Avoiding imposter syndrome and the other BS false lies that will try to hold you back from stepping into the spotlight.

- How to step into the spotlight without feeling like a phony or know-it-all

- How to fast track success by modeling or "hacking" success without feeling like a copycat

- How to go against the grain of your traditional or conservative industry without being seen as a complete maverick

- How to overcome imposter syndrome by showing up authentically.

Rumors and Reality:

- You may be thinking that industry wide recognition is for the young, rich, and beautiful, but the truth is that true experts come from a place of service and your age, income, and looks have nothing to do with it.

- You may be thinking that your industry is different and that marketing yourself as an expert just won't work, but the truth is that this process works even in the most conservative industries.

- You may be thinking that this process won't work for you, but the truth is that it will!

Introduction

Were you ever the new kid in school?

My dad was in the US Air Force for over 25+ years, so I grew up with constant 'new kid in school' syndrome. (That's not really a syndrome, I just made it up to prove a point.)

Most people don't know this about me, but I was born in England and didn't move to the states full time until I was about nine years old. Both of my little brothers were born overseas too. One brother was born in England, like me, and the other was born in Germany.

On one hand, growing up an "Air Force Brat" and moving every couple years was really exciting. We had a new adventure before us all the time! On the other hand, it was a total drag.

Here's what is a drag about being the new kid in school:
- You never know if your school clothes are 'cool' for the region you live in.
- You don't know who to hang out with and who is bad news.

- You feel ostracized and alone on that first day when you walk into the school and everyone knows each other.
- It's awkward finding kids to eat lunch with at first.

Here's what cool about being the new kid:

- If you were unpopular at the old school, you have a new chance to change.
- As a kid, you get to experience places and people very few others (including grown adults) get to experience in their entire life.
- You become adept at change and nothing throws you off.
- You get to reset the terms for who you are, who your friends are, and what you're about.

I think used to think that being the new kid all the time was super annoying. But, now as an adult and a business owner, I'm glad that I had that experience because it has helped me overcome moments of self doubt and 'imposter syndrome.'

Just like being the new kid in school, being the new expert on the scene in your industry can often result in similar thoughts:

What will people say or think when you show up like *that?*

If you do show up and step up, will people take you seriously?

What I found from being the perpetual new kid is that people will respect you if you show up authentically and as yourself.

When I tried to fit in with the cool kids and wear clothes that weren't my style, it showed on my face. I looked and felt uncomfortable and like a fraud.

When I wore what I want and showed up authentically, I gained acceptance.

The same is true as a business owner.

When I try to fit into someone else's mold, I feel uncomfortable and it shows.

When I show up as myself (the good, the bad, and the ugly), I feel comfortable and it shows.

Show Up Authentically to Avoid Imposter Syndrome

One of the insights that I share in my webinars and at my events is how to hack success by modeling those that are successful. If your business is struggling, it's easier and faster to invest in coaching or training by someone who has been there, done that, and been victorious versus trying to figure it out on your own.

But, coaching and training is a starting point or a foundation from which you need to build your own business upon taking what is different about you and infusing your own style and substance.

When I decided that I wanted to change my business model from being a marketing service provider to being an information and insights provider as a speaker and consultant, I took my own advice and hired the best in the business. I was trained by the world's best at Speaking Empire. I joined the legendary Dan Kennedy's organization GKIC (now the NO BS Inner Circle) and was one of a handful of Certified Magnetic Marketing Advisors for a few years. I was even trained by an Emmy award winning TV producer on how to be a great TV show host and guest because I knew it would help me on podcasts, radio shows, and TV segments.

I invested in myself, absorbed all the information, practiced and trained on their proven techniques, and once I had the basics down, I added my own unique approach to everything that I had learned from the best.

Now I get lots of phone calls from other business coaches and consultants who want to know my secret to success. They call and ask me to send them my pricing sheet, sign up for my webinars to hack my flow, and subscribe to my email list and Facebook group just to see what I send to my community.

But, here's what's wrong with that approach: how I run my business is different from how they should run their business because they have a specialness and uniqueness that is inherent to only them...and so do I.

Also, there is more to it then what is seen on the surface. There are reasons why my prices are set where they are, there are reasons why I have each slide in my webinar, there are reasons why I share my unique personal stories with my email list.

To become known as the go-to-expert in your business, you will need to consult with and be trained by the best, yes! But you will also need to reveal what makes you unique and add that to a solid foundation of training and advice.

Showing up as your authentic self and not just copy/pasting what your competition does is key to avoiding feeling like an imposter.

I describe what I do as a consultant to Rising Influencers as being a producer. Much like a musician has a song in their heart, there are foundational truths to music that need to be learned. Once the foundation is mastered, and the song idea is birthed, a music producer is brought in to pull out the best and refine it with the musician.

Boss Women Rock: It works!

April Caldwell
Trail Blazers Tribe
Money Boss

Jen: This chapter is on overcoming limiting beliefs about the way that things are always done and finding the courage and having the self- belief that you can do it, that you can transition yourself out of an industry maybe that you weren't completely 100% in love with or a job that you weren't in love into this new way of being in business. So, why don't you just take it from the top, April, and just tell me where you were and what epiphany or pivotal moment did you have that made you decide to leap and go your own way?

April: I actually made a couple of leaps. My first leap was from corporate into becoming a independent financial advisor. So, I went from having a steady job in the financial industry, very secure, and decided that I wanted more. I had my Master's Degree and other degrees and I had a lot of experience. I just didn't feel like I was doing what I was meant to do, and it wasn't being appreciated. In the corporate structure, it was very hard to get promoted, very hard to be recognized. Back then, it was very much like a boy's club, and even some of my female bosses, they were scared for their jobs. They were afraid that I'm gonna come after their jobs. It just really was an environment that I was unhappy in.

April: I made the leap to leave corporate America and become a business owner being a financial advisor and loved it. My passion has always been to help women, and so I went into this with the plan to help women. So I did that for 10 years and then I got to the point to where I knew there had to be more. I wasn't doing everything that I could to help others, to help other women, and made the second leap to rebrand, to have what little time I had with any structure and support and back office help to go out on my own to be a money coach.

Jen: Tell us about why you feel inspired to coach women in particular about issues related to money?

April: That really goes back to how I was raised and how I saw the women in my life handle money and be controlled by money. I tell the story about my mamaw a lot. She and my grandfather were married for 50 plus years, and they hated each other. And she stayed because she could not financially support herself without him. And I watched that with her, I watched that with my aunt, I watched that with my step-mom. They were not in positions where they could support themselves and be independent, and therefore, their happiness and their life was controlled by other people. I knew I never wanted to be in that position. So, my passion was to learn everything that I could and then make sure I help others do the same.

Jen: You were about to mention how you went out on your own, you left all the support, and you are using your message and your brand as you used that as, I guess, one of the starting points. How did you come up with the platform that you stand on?

April: So, are you talking about like my mission statement or are you talking about Trail Blazers?

Jen: Yes. Your brand. My opinion is that a lot of people think your brand is what you look like, what your logo is like and photo shoot and what your color scheme is. But to me, your brand is what you stand for and what you stand against. It's your message, and the difference that you're trying to make and your movement. You have a really strong one, right? You've got your Trail Blazers tribe, which we can talk about in a moment. How did you come up with the direction for your message and your platform, your brand?

April: I knew that I wanted to work with women because of my past. I knew that there was a missing piece. I knew that most people that were financial advisors were men, and I saw a need. I saw that women want to work with women. And I wanted to do something that was fun. If I was going to dedicate my life to this, I wanted to have fun and so I started doing women's events to promote myself and brand myself and get my business out there. And by doing women's events, that's who I attracted, that's who I work with, and then they referred me to more women. So, it was just really finding what I loved to do and being able to do that.

Jen: What kind of support or pushback did you get when you decided to leave the traditional way of doing things of a financial advisor and go off on your own as a women's money coach?

April: Oh my gosh. It was so funny. So a lot of pushback that I got was pity. Like everybody felt kind of sorry, like I was making this huge mistake. They were trying to talk me out of ruining my career, ruining my life. They couldn't see it. So, I got people telling me that it wasn't gonna work, that I couldn't do it, that I was making a mistake.

April: I had a few supporters, and of course, my husband has always been a huge supporter of what I've done. But people that I love and cared about and had been in business with for 10 years were telling me I was wrong.

Jen: Wow. So, you had all these people that you had been working with or been in business with for years telling you that you're wrong, and you have the support of your husband, which is great. What did you have to decide about yourself and believe about yourself to give you the courage to see your vision through?

April: I'm a competitive person, and if someone tells me I can't do something, I am going to show you that I can. No one's going to tell me no. It took a lot. I knew that these people, these naysayers, were wrong. I knew that. I knew that these people that had been in business for themselves on the traditional side for longer than I have are still in the same place. So, I had to recognize that, and I had to recognize that I had something different, that there was a need, that there was something special about this thing that I was creating that I could do this.

Jen: Right. And I think what I've seen happen is that you built a community of people that support you. Tell us a little bit about Trail Blazers?

April: Trail Blazers is different than anything I've seen or anything that I've created. I did women's events for years before Trail Blazers on the traditional side. And Trail Blazers is something that has ... it's taken on a life of its own. It's not about me, it's not even about what I do, it's about these women that are coming together and connecting, and it's not networking, it's not business referrals. It is about a true community.

April: It's these women that want more and are supporting each other not only at the events, not only online, but in real life.

They are showing up for each other. They are opening their offices on a Sunday afternoon to see a patient or coming to somebody's house to help them when they're sick. That's what Trail Blazers is about. It's about these women, no matter what we're going through or what stage we are in life, that we will support each other.

Jen: I love it. What is next on the horizon for Trail Blazers maybe in the next year or two? Also give us a look to the future, five to ten years down the road, what you want it to be? Tell me what's on the immediate horizon?

April: On the immediate horizon, I would like to see more women. I'd like to see more women coming to Trail Blazers, becoming a part of it. I'd like to see it grow. I'd like to see more women connecting with each other. I don't know if that looks like more frequent events. I don't want there to be a hundred women in a room. I think that we will lose some of what we have created. It might be more events and smaller groups, it might be hitting more areas, it might be something that we ... it might be something that we find a way to still do this online. I just want to see it get bigger.

Jen: Okay. And then what about future down the road? Where are you looking to go? Is Trail Blazers separate from April, the money coach, or similar?

April: Yeah, I guess I do see Trail Blazers and April Caldwell The Money Coach separately. I think that Trail Blazers is definitely a tool, it's a branding tool, it's a marketing tool. It's something that I do that I don't see I will get a lot of clients out of. It's more about building the kind of community I want to be a part of. And then April Caldwell, money coach, is more like my business, how I profit from my passion.

Jen: Okay. So, tell us about where April Caldwell, The Money Coach is headed?

April: I had a recent shift, so maybe a couple of months ago, I embraced virtual coaching. When before, I thought, "Oh no, nobody wants to have their money coach doing this online. They want to be in person." So, I shifted that, and now I see April Caldwell, Money Coach, going global, helping women around the world get straight with their money and not be limited to a regional area.

Jen: I love it. Any words of advice for another woman who might be reading this book, and they have some objections and naysayers that are holding them back from taking their leap? Anything that you could recommend to them to either make it easier or ... I know it's not easy, but what would you say to them?

April: I would say, first, and this is going to be probably from left field, but first I would listen to them. If you're looking to start your own business, expand, do something different, you want to look at all the pros and cons. You want to make sure you have a solid plan. The things that they're telling you, don't be afraid of them, you need to look at them and see if there's any validity to it, and how you can fix that. And then once you've done your due diligence and you take what they throw at you, and you make what you have even better, then you stop listening. And then you start listening to those that love you and support you, and you continue doing what you need to do.

Results Wrap Up:

If you had a process to follow that would empower you to overcome self doubt and give you the courage to step into the spotlight do you think you could be successful?

Yes! You can. To get started, you just need to take the Next Steps:

Take Action:

- ❏ Write down what unique experiences (good and bad) you have had that may benefit other people by helping them avoid a problem you experienced that they currently have or achieve a pleasure they want that you have attained.

- ❏ Select which business type best describes your current business (if you love it) or your future business (if you are building it.)
  - ❏ Coach - accountability

- ❑ Consultant - insights
- ❑ Counselor - guidance
- ❑ Trainer - technique
- ❑ Leader - vision
- ❑ Teacher - knowledge
- ❑ Entertainer - escape

❑ What unique gifts and talents do you have or can see yourself developing to bring the outcome your clients desire to your type of business?

Join the Boss Women Rock community and get access to bonus trainings, resources, and support from amazing people. Join us on Facebook at https://www.facebook.com/groups/ BossWomenRockSuccess

Chapter Three

Sharing your story in a way that is relatable, exciting, and moves people to action.

Stories sell. If you want to go from best kept secret to a sought after expert, you will need to be able to tell your story in a way that is interesting and entertaining to your audience <u>and moves them to action.</u>

A word of caution: there are a lot of dramatic, rags to riches stories that the internet gurus use in their presentations to pull on the heartstrings of their audience. Our goal is not to emotionally manipulate people or to make this all about us. Our goal is to shorten the know-like-trust factor and connect with our audience so we can spread our message and serve them.

Without letting people into your life and relating to them, you will have a much harder time finding your tribe and building a community of customers, clients, and patients that will do business with you.

Gains:

- How to turn your tragedies into triumphs without being overly dramatic
- How to connect on a personal level so you can shorten the know-like-trust cycle

- How to make your personal story relatable in your business

Rumors and Reality:

- You may be thinking that you aren't famous enough to have others care about your story. But the truth is, that right now, someone somewhere in the world is praying for a breakthrough that only you can give them.

- You may be thinking that the world doesn't care or need to hear about what you've overcome or learned the hard way, but the truth is that there are legions of people that need your help.

- You may be thinking that you need to be a professional writer to tell good stories, but the truth is you just need a fill-in-the-blanks template to follow. I'll make this easy and give it to you in a moment...

Stories have probably been a part of your life from the very beginning. When you were a baby your mother or father or another loved one held you in their arms and read you a story. Stories are used to ignite the imagination and to connect us on an emotional level.

As a business owner or expert, stories are a powerful business building tool you can use to connect with your potential clients on an emotional level. It is an important factor in your success.

Even if you are not a professional writer or gifted storyteller, you can learn how to connect with an audience through storytelling by following a simple formula. Let's break it down.

Stories have a few things in common. First they have a hero. The hero is the main character of the story and is typically dynamic, but flawed. A good story won't let this hero skate through life unchallenged, though. A good story will throw this hero some curveballs and problems. The bigger the problem, the more exciting the plot.

This hero with a problem will typically want something. There may be a girl he wants to win the heart of, a treasure to unearth, or a tournament of champions to win.

But, the issue is that this hero who wants this big reward, doesn't quite know how to make it happen. They may stumble around with awkward encounters with the girl, struggle to find the hidden gold, or get beaten time and time again in the championship playoffs.

So, the hero only has one choice: find a guide to help them get what they want.

In our business stories, you are not the hero. Your client is the hero. You are the guide.

Your job as the guide is to develop a plan that the hero can follow with your help to get the outcome they long for and to avoid the pitfalls that lay ahead.

Pitfalls may include enemies and roadblocks that are set to destroy their plan. In business enemies may include the competition, industry norms, bad information, or unforeseen events.

Let's look at how you can use stories to build your income, influence, and impact.

My Story: The day I gave up "Good on Paper"

I laid on the gurney in the ER with a throbbing pain in my side and a surgeon telling me I had a tumour.

How can this be I asked? Just moments ago I was at a business networking event, and now here I am wondering why this was happening to me and had my life really mattered?

You see I had been blindly checking off boxes and doing what was expected of me for 15 years, moving towards a "secure future" only to find out it's very shallow once you get there.

"Go to college so you can get a good job."

"Buy a sports car and a house in Florida with a pool."

"Don't stop climbing that corporate ladder until you reach the top."

Sure, our folks mean well when they tell us these things, but once I earned a master's degree, landed a 6-figure job, and bought a house in Florida with a pool out back and a red sports car parked in front, I realized I still wasn't fully living.

But, for most people that have the guts to leave the security of the corporate world and make the leap into entrepreneurship, the results are dismal. They are barely making it on a take home pay of $40,000 per year and 80% fail in the first 18 months...

That's barely enough to cover their mortgage, much less make a difference in the world.

Didn't my life have a bigger meaning than collecting a paycheck? Couldn't I use my gifts and talents to make an impact?

It was the day that everything changed for me and I decided to give up the good to go for great. Leave it to a health scare to create a life changing moment.

So, when just 4 years later, I unlocked the secret to building a business that runs without me in the day-to-day AND makes a great income, the clients came calling and opportunities came out of the woodwork.

Would you like to know what I found out? Are you interested in how I was able to turn my creative gifts and talents into a thriving business while I was regaining my health, spending time with my new husband, and traveling the country and world?

Boss Women Rock covers the key concepts I've used to build a thriving business based on what I know, not just what I do. So you can do the same thing.

The Epiphany

I was sitting in the front row of the Entrepreneur magazine conference in Dallas watching Barbara Corcoran speak to a crowd of hundreds of eager business owners. There were dozens of round tables at the foot of the stage each person with their gaze fixed on Barbara and hanging on her every word.

My husband and I had travelled to the conference when I started my first version of a marketing consultancy. We were there to hear Barbara speak primarily, and meet new prospective clients secondarily. But, what happened that day changed my life forever.

As we sat through hour upon hour of presentations from business leaders sharing their tips on how to grow a business, I realized that we all had missed the answer that was right in front of us.

I looked at how Barbara was using her clout and fame to get on a stage, and I thought, wow, she is amazing.

Here she is up on a stage with all eyes fixed on her and she's solving the #1 marketing problem on the planet- getting attention. Plus, she was being paid to do it! She was being paid to market her business.

Then, I noticed that her team was selling her books in the lobby. And another lightbulb went off. AHA! She's taken what she knows and put it into a format that can help millions of people. She's systemized what she knows.

I was doing the math and figured that she probably made at least $50,000 for the speaking gig, and sold another $3,000 in books that day. Plus, the PR for her brand and business was invaluable.

But the craziest part was that she was only there for about an hour that day! When she was done, she hopped on her jet and travelled on to the next destination.

The book did the selling for her! She was able to position herself as an expert, write a book once and get paid for it over and over again!

That's when I realized that I didn't want to build a traditional business the way most people do it selling consulting by the hour, I wanted to do what Barbara did and sell my knowledge as a speaker, author, and coach.

And so that's what I did...

And I did this all by focusing on TWO things...

Positioning myself as an expert and creating systems so the business could help more people, women in business to be specific.

If you're like me and you're ready to make a bigger impact, elevate your influence, and generate the income you deserve, then welcome to Boss Women Rock.

Boss Women Rock : It Works!

Stephanie Lincoln
Fire Team Whiskey
Boss Women Rock Member

Jen: All right, Stephanie. Thanks for participating in the Boss Women Rock book. And I'm excited to have you as one of the featured Boss Women. And I just want to start by having you tell us why you started Fire Team Whiskey.

Stephanie: I'll be as brief as possible on this because it's kind of a long story. But I started Fire Team Whiskey based a culmination of observations, and experiences I had over the last 19 years of my life. I wore the uniform for 10 years, and after I got out of the military, I feel like I went right back in because they hired me to start a mental health program for the Florida Army National Guard. This was just a year after I got out uniform.

Stephanie: For the next nine years of my life I worked in military medical. I was embedded with military and medical. I was embedded with units, and just observing the day-to-day health, and physical fitness of the military members. I was asked to do a lot of work with the Air Force, the Army Reserves, the Air Force Reserves. I traveled all over the country speaking with the higher ups in the chain of command about the medical needs and the behavioral health needs of our service members.

Stephanie: Over this time I observed a really dramatic decline in the military member's health and fitness. It just astounded me because when I enlisted in 1999 if I would have shown up on a drill hall floor holding a 20 ounce energy drink in one hand, and being overweight, and looking really unprofessional in my uniform, and three doughnuts in the other hand, my platoon sergeant probably would have physically assaulted me. It was a given at that time that you always had to look good in your uniform. You had to look sharp and fit. You would never be caught carrying around food like that. If you were a service member that smoked you had to go and hide.

Stephanie: Over the years I've just noticed sitting down with these young soldiers, that at 19 and 20 years old they had high blood pressure, high cholesterol, and were on several medications. They were flagged that they couldn't run because they had knee pain or back pain and were 60 pounds overweight. I was just astounded by how many there were that fell into this category. It just did not look like that when I was in the military back in the late '90s, early 2000s.

Jen: So, what has changed?

Stephanie: I mean, obviously we've been at war for 17-18 years
                now and I think just also our society at large has fall-
                en into this complacency with what's the most conve-
                nient, and fast, and easy ... and kind of like this quick
                I need to get this now, and I don't care if it's healthy
                for me, go through the fast food restaurant, Uber Eats
                kind of society. Rather than being very thoughtful
                about how everything impacts our health. Whether
                it be our stress levels, and what we eat on a daily basis
                and how much we move, and how much we sit on our
                butts, and play games or binge on six hours of Netflix
                a day.

Stephanie: It's just become a complacent society, and it's trick-
                led into our military. People don't realize that 54% of
                our uniformed military is overweight, or obese. So,
                in my journey, I just decided to kind of combine the
                things that I love about mental health, and behav-
                ioral change, with the things that I love about fitness
                and nutrition, and offer these programs to our mili-
                tary members, veterans, and first responders because
                they're the ones whose lives are on the line. If they're
                not fit, then their lives can be on the line. On any giv-
                en day if they are challenged, and they have to run,
                or move fast, or lift something fast, or lift their own
                body weight. If they aren't fit or healthy enough to do

that, then they could lose their lives..and in turn other people could lose their lives.

Jen: Let's talk about how you're reaching these military and first responders. How are you getting your message in front of them? How are you making them care? Because if they don't care on their own, how are you making them get it?

Stephanie: Well, we have quite a few approaches with that. First approach is infiltrating, and getting in with the military leaders. Because I know as a former military leader how frustrating it is. I was the body fat officer in my very first unit as a young lieutenant. I was in charge of this. Brand new out of OCS, I was thrown in my battalion, which had about 300 people in it. And said, "All right, here you go. You're a brand new officer. You're in charge of the health and fitness of our entire unit." And I know firsthand, just how frustrating that is for a military leader to have so many soldiers in their ranks out of shape, and not meeting the standards.

Stephanie: And what can you do? I mean, you can discipline them. You can talk to them. You can reason with them. But really what it comes down to is being a good example. You have that theme of lead from the front, right? Getting in with military leaders, and I've done several talks in front of military leaders with major units here in Florida about this issue, about how it is their responsibility. And they are responsible because this would affect the mission, right?

Stephanie: If we're on a mission, and I'm in charge of a platoon full of soldiers, and half that platoon is not fit, then that could compromise my mission. Right? Emphasizing with them, this is your responsibility. And you really do need to emphasize this with your soldiers. Not only lead from the front, and make sure that you're keeping your own health and fitness in check, and showing by example. But also encouraging your soldiers that this is a priority, and it really is ... It's not just, "Oh, you're just overweight." It comes down to, "Your life could be on the line, and in turn your battle buddy's lives could be on the line because you didn't do what you needed to do on a daily basis to take care of this issue."

Jen: You're basically using speaking, and influencer marketing to get to the leaders of the community. Where do you want to take Fire Team Whiskey? What's your bold plan? What's your big vision?

Stephanie: Big vision is to have my program be provided to every single reserve component, service member in the United States. So, when you come back from your basic training, boom, you get a package. You know, as soon as you get home, so you can keep that momentum. You got in great shape in boot camp, right? Like, you didn't have a choice. But for the reserve components, I have such a passion for them because they come home, and they only go to drill once a month. But they're supposed to be held to active duty physical fitness and body fat standards.

Stephanie: They have jobs. They own businesses. They have kids. They're going to school full-time. You know, this isn't their full-time job. Yet, tomorrow they can get orders, and be in Iraq in a couple weeks. Right? So, what's the difference? The difference is they don't have any resources. So, I think it's just doing the right thing as far as the military is concerned, is to provide realistic resources to our reserve component members. That's why I created the programs that I did because they can be done by anyone, anywhere, literally on any time frame.

Stephanie: So, you can work on shift work at night. I have military members in Iraq doing my program right now. I have Navy service members underway on a ship who are doing my program right now. We've proven that this program can be done by anyone, anywhere, and it can help them meet military body fat, and fitness standards within 60 days of starting our programs.

Jen: It sounds like you really know who your audience is. You know what your message is. You've got this bigger movement that you're creating, and leading, and taking the charge on. And you're recruiting people to get onboard this change, this transformation that you're trying to instill in the military, and first responder community.

Jen: Tell us about the community you've built to rally around the Fire Team Whiskey mission, tell us a little bit about that. How in your marketing, and in your business growth are you using building a tribe, or a community?

Stephanie: I love that you asked this, Jen. Because I think that there is a lot of great products out there, and programs, and they miss the mark on this. And this is what it's all about, if you don't spark a fire within your customers, or your potential customer's hearts, and kind of get them to be your biggest cheerleaders, you're always gonna struggle. Because you're just, you're always pitching to a cold market, and they have no investment in you, or your product, or what you're doing.

Stephanie: I named my company Fire Team for a reason. And that is the concept. A fire team is the smallest element in the military. It's you, and four, or five people who

do everything together. These are the people that become your family. You eat, sleep, and breathe, and do
everything together. You see the best, and the worst
of them. And you have a mission together. No man is
left behind. So, we instill that concept in everything
we do.

Stephanie: So, the people who have done our program feel like
this is their family now. And they could never leave
this family. And they're so excited, and empowered
by it that they share it with their friends, and their
families. We have whole families who end up enlisting
in our program because one member of their family
started. So, maybe the one member of their family is
a military member, and maybe had such success, and
they love it so much that they bring their wife in. That
they bring their dad in, that they bring their mom in,
that they bring their mother-in-law in. We've had this
happen. So, it is about creating that family concept,
that team concept, that we're in this together.

Stephanie: And that's how we approach everything we do. It's not
just like, "Hey, I have a product. If you like it, maybe
you might buy it." It's, "Hey, join us." We say list enlist. We don't even say, "Hey, buy now." We say, "Enlist
with us. Enlist in our Fire Team. Join our Fire Team.
Become a part of our family."

Jen:

If you have family members, and team members on ships, and submarines, and at war, or in the homeland. What specific tools are you using, and strategies are using to communicate, and keep that fire lit among everyone?

Stephanie:

I think this is the important part of it. I mean, you have to approach it from all angles. You have to keep your members engaged, and you have to challenge them. You have to produce new content every single day. And also encourage your team members to produce content for you. Some of the most valuable discussions that we've had as groups have been from our just Fire Team members. Bringing things up on our group forums, and asking questions, or making a suggestion about something.

Stephanie:

The reason why we offer our program now on the USB Dog Tag drives is because it was one of our Fire Team member's ideas. Always be just like open to kind of encouraging that group content building. Ask a question, get a discussion going. Don't just say, "Oh, here's our new product." You know, "Here, here's the link. Buy now." "Oh, here's another product. Here, buy now."

Stephanie:

It has to be all about keeping them engaged in the topics that they're interested in. Obviously, we're in health and fitness, so pretty much everything we talk about is health and fitness. And just continuing to produce new content, and rallying that passion, and motivation on a daily basis.

Jen: If you could go back in time, and change one thing about your start as a business owner, and an entrepreneur with Fire Team Whiskey, what would it be?

Stephanie: The one thing that I probably would have changed was ... I would have had maybe a better handle on where our focus was gonna be. I think when we first started our vision was too broad. We were like okay, we're gonna appeal to the keto market. We're gonna appeal to the weight loss market. We're gonna appeal to the corporate market. We're gonna appeal to gyms with our bars. We're gonna get into health businesses...It was just ... We were all over the place.

Stephanie: Like, we had like 30 areas that we were focusing on. And obviously when you do that, you distill your focus. You can't focus 100% on 300 different things. I think that's what I would change. I would have just come in from the get-go focused on the two things that we're focused on now pretty much. We've had to come back, and reset, and refocus, and just get rid of everything else.

Stephanie: Yeah, those projects would be wonderful. And those are like pie in the sky future things that we would like to focus on, and get involved in, and get going with. But I think it would have been smarter from the get-go to just say, "All right, we are doing our .22 Caliber program with military members, veterans, and first responders." Boom, that's it. And then, "Hey, we're gonna have our bars listed on Amazon."

Stephanie: Those are just the two things we need to focus on right now. That way we're not distilling down our energy, which is what happened. And I think it caused us a lot of grief in the beginning because of that.

Jen: Yeah, it's one of the big things that I preach, is you have to know exactly who your market is. And when a business owner tells me it's for "anyone," I almost jump out of my skin because I can see the waste of time and money that they're about to embark on. When you say that your business is for "anyone," it doesn't work. It has to be so specific. And you have to be able to get inside the mind of your client, your potential client, so that when you create your marketing messages, you can communicate with them. They don't feel like you're talking at them. They feel like you get them. And that this is like a no brainer decision for them to jump onboard your community, your tribe, buy your products, attend your events.

Stephanie: Yeah. And I think that, that was a big struggle for us when we first started. You're always gonna get negative feedback. So, that's another takeaway that I just wish I could share with other budding entrepreneurs. Is you're gonna get negative feedback. I literally had people say to me, "Well, you really shouldn't discount civilians. It seems like you just don't like civilians. What about me?" And that's hard to take. That's hard to hear. That's hard to be told.

Stephanie: I literally was in a meeting last week with a potential investor, (and by the way he's definitely not investing.) He told me for an hour basically how much he hated my company. And how he hated the logo, and it shouldn't have bullets in it, and it's offensive, and it's too focused on the military. He was just like breaking down every single thing in my business that he hated, and you're gonna get a lot of that.

Jen: I think it's actually good. I think it's actually good when your brand is repelling. Like a magnet it needs to do two things. It needs to attract the right people, and it needs to repel the wrong. Do you agree?

Stephanie: Yes. Yes.

Jen: So, congratulations because it sounds like you are on the right track.

Stephanie: And then being okay with that. I mean, you really do. And I just sat there, and took it, and left that meeting and I went to my tribe. I went to my team, my Fire Team, and said, "Hey guys, just FYI, the things that I love about this business, and the things that I know that you guys value, you know, I just met with a potential investor. He hates. And he doesn't like the fact that we spend time with you guys. He doesn't like the fact that we coach you. He doesn't like the fact that we have bullets in our logo, et cetera, et cetera." And you can get that immediate feedback from the people who are your brand ambassadors, and they all say, "Well, F him." You know? "We love it. We love Fire Team. We're gonna share it even more just because of that guy."

Stephanie: If you go back to your people, and you go back to your target audience, you're gonna continue to kind of get that positive feedback. But there is always gonna be haters out there that will try and take you in another direction.

Jen: Yep. And like I said, I think that's a sure sign of success. So, what's next? What's next for Fire Team Whiskey?

Stephanie: Well, Fire Team Whiskey, we literally just launched to the public two months ago. Really, like you said

Jen, we are just building our tribe. We're building our brand ambassadors. It really is a mainly word of mouth business right now. And I think that's why ... Even though I think it's taking longer to build, which is frustrating. You know, you want to see those sales go up, up, up, up. But I think the way that we're doing it because the sales are coming from genuine people who are going to be a part of our team, and our gonna be brand ambassadors, and getting kind of ... Getting those additional sales for us without us having to pay for any marketing. That's what we're focused on right now.

Stephanie: I think what works for us as a brand is that we are very specific to who we're speaking to. We're gonna build our tribe. Build our brand ambassadors, and just build exponentially. Explode exponentially from there.

Results Wrap Up:

If you had a template to follow that would empower you to spread your message and create a movement do you think you could be successful?

Yes! You can. To get started, you just need to take the Next Step Action.

Take Action:

Write down the key breakthroughs or epiphany moments you have had in your life that made you want to change your life or business:

How did you overcome the challenges?

How can you relate this to your audience?

How do you think you could leverage your gifts and talents to get this message to others?

What outcome can you provide to others that is:

Emotional (thoughts & feelings based)_____

Functional (results oriented)_____

Dimensional (time based)_____

Fill in the blanks to get the rough idea of your story outlined and then sit down to draft your full story:

A character (your customer/client/patient)_____ has a problem (what keep them up at night) _____.

They meet a Guide (you)_____ who gives them a plan _____ ____ to save them from failure (thing they're most afraid of)_____ _____ and ensures success (thing they want)__ _____.

Join the Boss Women Rock community and get access to bonus trainings, resources, and support from amazing people. Join us on Facebook at https://www.facebook.com/groups/ BossWomenRockSuccess

Chapter Four

Connecting with an audience that will actually care about your message and support your mission

Becoming a sought after expert will require a few things. First, it will require that you're in it for the long game. Experts are successful because they have built trust over time. If you're looking for a silver bullet solution or get rich quick scheme, this is not the approach for you.

Second, it will require that you stand for something and stand against something else. You will need to wage a war on the injustice or wrong-doers that you are battling against.

Third, it will require that you rally the troops around you and build a community of like-minded supporters to champion your cause.

With those key elements in place, you will be readied for the battle of your life. This will become your life's work.

Gains:
- How to build a team of supporters so you don't have to do everything yourself without hiring a bunch of employees

- How to create change in an industry that embraces status quo and "we've always done it like that" mentality

- How to leverage your credibility and influence to make a lasting impact for more fulfillment in your business and life

Rumors and Reality:

- You may be thinking that one person can't make real change, but the truth is that they can, just look at Dr. Martin Luther King Jr!

- You may be thinking that your industry is stuck in it's old ways and will never change, but the truth is that change is inevitable, it just needs to be championed. Just look at the fall of Blockbuster and the rise of Netflix.

- You may be thinking that being a Rising Influencer is too challenging, but the truth is you just need an approach you can follow and some key contacts.

Introduction

I'm an introvert. Really, it's true! I am! A lot of people are surprised when I reveal this little known fact because my business runs on speaking, media appearances, and training people in groups.

As an introvert, my natural inclination is to hide behind my computer. I avoid local networking events like the plague. It's not because I don't like people or am shy, it's just because I recharge by being alone. I can think clearer on my own, then in a group or at an event.

But, the reality of the situation is that I will need other people to help me accomplish my mission. I am on a mission to turn the entrepreneurial failure rate of 80% upside down and ensure that each person that I come into contact with gets the truth about what it really takes to run a profitable business.

As I mentioned in Chapter One, my rally cry is

Because Your Message is Powered by Profit™

When I wake up in the morning and my feet hit the ground, I know exactly what my purpose is and feel energized and inspired.

But, the reality is, I can't do this alone. In order to create success for myself, I have to make it about other people. In the words of Zig Ziglar, "I can have everything I want in life, if I just help enough other people get what they want in life." I have to include other people and I need other people to help carry the flag.

When you have a greater purpose to your business and make it about helping others, your mission will become bigger than you.

Boss Women Rock: It Works!

Lea Haben Woodford
SmartFem

Jen: Tell us about SmartFem.

Lea: My goal with the SmartFem Network is to bring back
          integrity and authenticity to the book industry and the
          speaking industry, because I just see a lot of bad informa-
          tion, old information, and stuff that is just BS.

Jen: Was this a pivotal moment or an epiphany that you had, or
          was it just a gradual realization?

Lea: When I wrote my first book, I realized that I knew noth-
          ing about the book industry and I couldn't find anybody
          who did. So I decided to create a conference and go after
          the traditional book publishers and the book distributors.
          How do I get my book in the airport? How do I get it into
          the Barnes and Noble? That information is not out there
          for speakers and consultants. When I wrote my first book
          I called one of the top PR companies in New York, and
          they said it's going to be $7500 per month, three month
          minimum and there are no guarantees. I just thought,
          "Wow, I'm in the media. We've got to change this. And we
          have to bring credibility back." I've just seen alot people
          get so burned who spent $10,000- $20,000 on books, and

they have a whole garage full and they don't know how to speak. I thought, "You know what, I'm going to create a conference that I want to go to and I'm going to bring in the real experts, because it's got to stop."

Jen: So I see there are two trains of thoughts that I'm seeing. I see one train of thought where authors are trying to make their money off the sale of their books and getting paid for speaking, and then on the other hand there is the train of thought where you're writing books just to build your credibility and build your business on the back end. What side of the fence are you on? What strategy do you go with?

Lea: You know, unless you're writing a book about Trump, you're probably not going to make any money at it. It is the vehicle for speaking, or getting business. That's how I see it. That's how I've always seen it. Yes, you'll make a little bit of money. For example, I'm speaking in Australia, they bought books and I shipped them off. I don't see that being a big money maker, but I do see it as a credibility build-er. Even when you speak for free, you can negotiate. "I'm going to waive my speaking fee, why don't I give you 400 books? Why don't you just pay for that?" There are ways to negotiate the sale of the book. For our TV show about book authors, we actually have a contest. The SmartFem dynamic book contest, and I was shocked. I had received about 150 books this year, Jen, and I'm looking for 10 and

I cannot believe how many books are so poorly written and not edited.

Lea: That's one of the other reasons I started it. I think that people have great intentions, but they don't know. I wanted to pool my resources, and my contacts, and my strategic partners to put better books out, but to help people avoid the pitfalls that so many fall into.

Jen: Yeah, I've picked up a couple, and you can almost tell right away when it's been one of those speak to write books, where they basically are just speaking into a recorder, transcribing it, slapping a cover on it, and then trying to sell it as a book. When I wrote my first book, I wrote it with two business partners, so I'm the co-author of it, it's called *Amplify Your Business*. When we wrote that book, we made a lot of mistakes at the beginning because we were basically trying to take old content that we had from blog posts and stuff like that, and reformat it into a book. I got frustrated because it took about three years to get it to the point where it was even salvageable, and I still hated it, so we ended up hiring an editor.

Jen: So does SmartFem help authors and experts and speakers and things with the actual book writing process?

Lea: Yes.

Lea: We do. In SmartFem Publishing, we're creating our own group. We have editors and a ghost writer, John Peregrine who's part of the group. I have a relationship with literary agents, who actually sponsor our conference. They too have had their business been affected by these so called book publishers and hybrid publishers and consultants who are going to help you write that book in 30 days. It's hurt their business too. They said, "We love what you're doing. And we want to help people." The problem is so many people fall for the really slick marketing campaign on Facebook, and the next thing you know $10,000 spent. At the end of the day, not only do they not have a good book, but often times, and this has happened to one of the members in our group, the rights to that book are gone, and now they have the rights to the next book that he wants to write, and we're trying to extricate him from that contract. A lot of people just don't really read contracts. There are a lot of people preying on them.

Lea: They're so excited about writing their first book, that they jump in with both feet, and they really don't know who they're in business with.

Jen: What I experienced doing it ourselves completely and not knowing what we were doing the first time around, was that we wasted three years of our lives, trying to do it ourselves. We should have just hired a professional from the beginning. Eventually, we hired a local editor, and copy editor and they helped us format it into real professional book that we're very proud of. In the end, I wish we would have saved ourselves the headache and saved ourselves the time and just hired someone to help us get there faster. I see the importance of that, because there is this gap in the market for self published authors that don't want to give away the rights to their entire intellectual property, but they also don't want to flounder around like I did for three years, and try to do it on their own.

Lea: What I realized was that if it was tough for me as a magazine publisher and being a media personality, it must be tough for others. I'm was talking to my celebrity clients like the founders of Barefoot Wines, and they too found themselves in this kind of predicament. Some of the celebrities that I've worked with have also fallen prey. Then I realized, there's a real need to bring back integrity into the book business. And that's when I sought after the professionals who really put it in the airports and the bookstores and the real literary agents. How do you get a book proposal? What if you want to do traditional publishing? I decided it was time to bring all those people in, and that's really why I created the conference. Speaking and book authors, they just go well together.

Jen: When book publishing first started you had to go with a publisher, you had to try and knock on somebody's door in New York City and land a publishing deal, and very few people could actually get their message out. Then the pendulum swung to the other side, and self publishing became available, but as we talked about there's major pitfalls and disasters to be avoided in self publishing and now it sounds like you swung it back the other way and maybe found the sweet spot between begging a publisher to write your book for you and doing it all on your own solo, it sounds like you hit that sweet spot, which is very needed.

Lea: The publishers have lost out too because of the charlatans and the slick marketing people. I think bringing in the real experts and I think for our audience, hearing it from the horse's mouth, here's how you need to write, here's what you need to do to get into the airports. A lot of people don't realize that despite the fact that you self published, you still can get into the book stores and into the airports.

Jen: Yeah, I don't think people know that.

Lea: No, and I didn't know that. That's why I'm so passionate about this. There are a lot of things that I didn't know, and I could share it, but that's not my wheelhouse, that's not my area of expertise. It makes more sense to bring in the experts. I'm staying in my lane because that's what I'm good at. And I'd much rather play in the sandbox with the people who know their stuff, live it, breathe it and can bring it.

Jen: What I've noticed from being involved in SmartFem, is that you're really building a community. It's not just another group where you're going to pop in and out and grab a tip or a trick there and then go on your way to the next group. It's really about relationships. Where do you want to take the SmartFem community? What's your big bold vision for this group of people that you're building?

Lea: I love entrepreneurism, I want to give them the tools. I think the conversations need to be global, and I'm working on global conversations and global events, because some of the stuff we're seeing here in the U.S. they're having those same issues in the UK and in Ireland, and obviously Australia as well. I think the conversations need to be more global. I believe that with Facebook, this is not a short term project. This is a really long passion of mine. It's not something that's just going to change overnight. We're building, and we're vetting everybody that comes into the group. I think that's what makes us different. We really care about our members, and it's a member-centric group, and I think that's something that's different and that's going to give us the longevity and the bandwidth.

Jen: Sometimes, when we're talking about building business, building a community is also known as building your audience. Because you've got television shows that need an audience, and you've got your books and programs and all these things that need to build an audience, do you recommend to other expert speaker, author, coaches, that they start thinking differently about what their audience means? Do you recommend that they take this approach in an effort to help build their business as well?

Lea: Well, I'll tell you how I came to this. I kind of fell into it a little bit. I've been working on the conference for a while, and I have a Facebook group, but I didn't start growing it until I did a Facebook live on Keto for beginners. I did a nine day egg fast, and I dropped nine pounds in nine days, and after, I did a Facebook Live. I had 17,000 people watching, and thousands of comments. I went, "Okay, wow. I'm missing something." I have a Facebook group and I am definitely not doing something right. And fortunately for us, SmartFem is an award-winning magazine, we've been around for a long time, and I went to one of my writer's and I said, "Hey, I need some help."

Lea: I brought her on to consult for us on how to build a group, and she kind of validated what I had always known. First of all, you never bet against Mark Zuckerberg. And the other thing is that's where Facebook can monetize. You've got to go where the money is. Follow the money. You and I talk about this. They can monetize groups that have engagement. That's when I really decided I'm going to build this group. She's helped me out with the structure and the guidelines. The other thing is, really vetting the group. Some of the large groups that I've seen and women entrepreneur groups, it's just a pitch fest and MLM's and there's no real engagement and there's no relationships. It's just look at me, look at me, look at me.

Lea: Our group is really about education, and empowerment and leveraging, and helping each other. I don't want to do it on my own. That's why I brought in the strategic partners that I did, because at the end of the day, I still have a magazine that I have to run, and three TV shows that I have to produce. I have a company to run and I can't do this by myself, and I'm not an expert on everything.

Lea: This is a long term love affair. And it really is about empowering women, because in 2009 I made a promise to my daughter that I would create something that would educate, empower, and inspire women, and SmartFem is more than just our conference and our magazine and our TV shows. I believe that we are a platform for women, and we give them a voice. That to me, the glass ceiling is still there for women and I want to see that gone in my lifetime.

Jen: I love it, me too. So let's talk about the role that the men are playing in SmartFem, because I know that SmartFem is for women, it's a movement that you're creating for women, but it has a lot of male supporters also, which I think is great. Talk about that a little bit if you wouldn't mind.

Lea: Sure. Well, first of all I bring in the best experts, and sometimes they're not women. I took a lot of flak last year, because I have men on my stage. These are all male ambassadors, and we still need men to take us to the table, and I bring in the best experts and I don't care if they're male, female, black, white, red, purple, polka-dot, if they're the experts, that's who I want.

Jen: Fantastic. What's the next step for someone that's reading this book to connect with SmartFem? Where should we send them?

Lea: Go to SmartFem.com, our magazine. Jen, you're going to be writing for us. I'm excited about that. You can check out any of our shows. We have three different shows. We're on the Roku, and Amazon Prime platform. Join our Facebook group, the SmartFem Entrepreneur Network. That is really where you're going to get to connect with people. I'm so proud of this group, Jen, because there's interaction. It's not just likes, but people generally support there, and they're doing business together, and they're building businesses together and that makes me really happy. That was the purpose of the group.

Results Wrap Up:

If you had a simple action plan to follow that would empower you to identify the bigger purpose for your business do you think you could be successful?

Yes! You can. To get started, you just need to take the Next Step Action.

Take Action:

What do you stand for?

What do you stand against?

What outdated norms are you trying to change?

What truth are you trying to reveal?

Join the Boss Women Rock community and get access to bonus trainings, resources, and support from amazing people. Join us on Facebook at https:// www.facebook.com/groups/BossWomenRockSuccess

Chapter Five

Start with the end in mind.
Build your primary business offer first for
maximum profitability and impact.

Becoming a sought after expert is an attractive idea mainly because it rings of promises of higher income, impact, and influence.

Based on my own experience and the experience of my clients and colleagues, those promises are basically true.

However, where the wheels fall off, so to speak, is primarily in the value that is exchanged.

It's almost impossible to become a highly sought after expert with discount, bargain prices and an exchange of time for money. The primary mindset shift that will need to take place is that what you do as a coach, consultant, or service based business that focuses on impacting other people's lives matters. That changing someone's life by improving their health, wealth, or relationships is a big deal!

If you as the expert don't value what you do enough to command your worth, then your customers and clients never will.

I have talked to numerous impact-driven experts who are so frustrated from not being able to maintain a profitable business. They know that what they do matters because they see the results their clients get. They are good at creating breakthroughs and mending broken businesses, bodies, behaviors, and lives. But they lack a clear strategy for how to price their services, products, courses, and programs.

Most of them just take a look at what the competition is charging and copy/paste the pricing on to their website and price sheets with total disregard and misunderstanding of if that company is even profitable!

Others just randomly pick a number out of thin air and call it a day. This typically happens when someone stops working for another company and goes solo because their "hourly rate as an entrepreneur is three times what it is as an employee."

This is a profit death trap. Let me explain in this chapter.

Gains:

- How to command a higher price for your services without losing your best clients and customers.

- How to provide so much value in your pricing that your competition becomes irrelevant and price shopping a thing of the past.

- How to weed out bad clients and prospects through effective pricing without feeling guilty.

Rumors and Reality:

- You may be thinking that your hourly rate is a reflection of your time and talent but the truth is that charging hourly rates is killing your business' profitability because you're trading time for money.

- You may be thinking that everyone in your industry charges hourly rates so you should too, but the truth is 80% of businesses go out of business in the first 18 months, so they're probably doing it wrong!

- You may be thinking that creating value-based pricing is tricky and complicated, but the truth is that by following my process, you too can move away from price shoppers and tire kickers and attract your ideal, perfect clients who will gladly pay your fees in exchange for the outcome you provide.

Introduction

Ana is an ARNP and Medical Director of a 5-month old (at the time of this writing) direct primary care business in Florida. Direct primary care cuts out the headache of dealing with insurance companies and complicated billing and provides fast, affordable and effective primary care and women's health services on a cash-pay monthly membership model.

Ana has been an ARNP for 18 years and is well known and loved so her trust factor is extremely high. But, in this new business model, Ana needed to be able to demonstrate the true value of the membership plan in a way that was easy for new potential patients to understand.

When Ana contacted me, her prices were listed on her website as $75 per month, but lacked a clear description of the true value her patients receive.

When I sat down with her she explained, "Jen, cash flow is so tight in my business right now. I'm waiting for $75 per month to come in from each patient, but I need a large infusion of revenue now. I need sales. How can I make this happen quickly?"

Using my Rising Influencer Profit Process™, I analyzed her business and found that just by changing her pricing structure, we could generate instant revenue in her business, and lots of it in a very short period of time.

I moved Ana to value based pricing and the results were extraordinary. Within 48 hours she was closing $950- $1,150 packages versus the $75 per month model.

Here's what Ana's pricing looks like after the makeover:

Basic	Deluxe	Premium
~~$900~~ **$750 / year** Or $75 per month (save $150 on annual)	~~$1140~~ **$950 / year** Or $95 per month (save $190 on annual)	~~$1,380~~ **$1150 / year** Or $115 per month (save $230 on annual)
No co-payments	No co-payments	No co-payments
Same day or next day extended appointments	Same day or next day extended appointments	Same day or next day extended appointments
Unlimited visits per month	Unlimited visits per month	Unlimited visits per month
Cell phone and video chat visits	Cell phone and video chat visits	Cell phone and video chat visits
Annual physical with comprehensive wellness evaluation	Annual physical with comprehensive evaluation- PLUS Free wellness labs	Annual physical with comprehensive evaluation- PLUS Free wellness labs
Quick response from provider or support staff by phone	Quick response from provider or support staff by phone	Quick response from provider or support staff by phone
Free lab draws	Free lab draws	Free lab draws
Availability to purchase most medications in the office	Availability to purchase most medications in the office	Availability to purchase most medications in the office
Nutrition and weight loss counseling	Nutrition and weight loss counseling	Nutrition and weight loss counseling
Hormone and adrenal assessments	Hormone and adrenal assessments	Hormone and adrenal assessments
One free vitamin B12 or B-lipo injection	Free B-lipo package (total of 4 injections)	Free B-lipo package (total of 4 injections)
	Discounts on supplements	Discounts on IV therapy
		Discounts on supplements
		Free door-to-door delivery on prescriptions and supplements
		Care for visiting, out-of-town family & friends

By moving away from flat rate pricing ($75 per month) and moving to value based pricing, Ana was able to clearly explain and demonstrate the value to her patients, make her competition irrelevant, and generate infusions of cash in her business almost overnight.

Ana Stauch
2 reviews
★★★★★ a week ago
"Jen, before hiring you I felt like I had lost control over the money in my business. I didn't really know what I should and should not do to grow. Now I am in complete control and actually enjoying the process. Plus, we're measuring our results everyday. Putting profit first and focusing on pricing has enabled us to generate more cash flow faster. It's only been a couple days and I see the difference financially! Plus, the strategies you created for me to generate leads are going to be really fun."

This same exercise in moving toward value based pricing could also be applied in a coaching or consulting business quite easily.

Here's an example of how I did it for a product I was selling from the stage at one of my own events. Dan Kennedy actually featured this in an article for his infamous NO BS Marketing Newsletter in 2017.

Boss Women Rock: It Works!

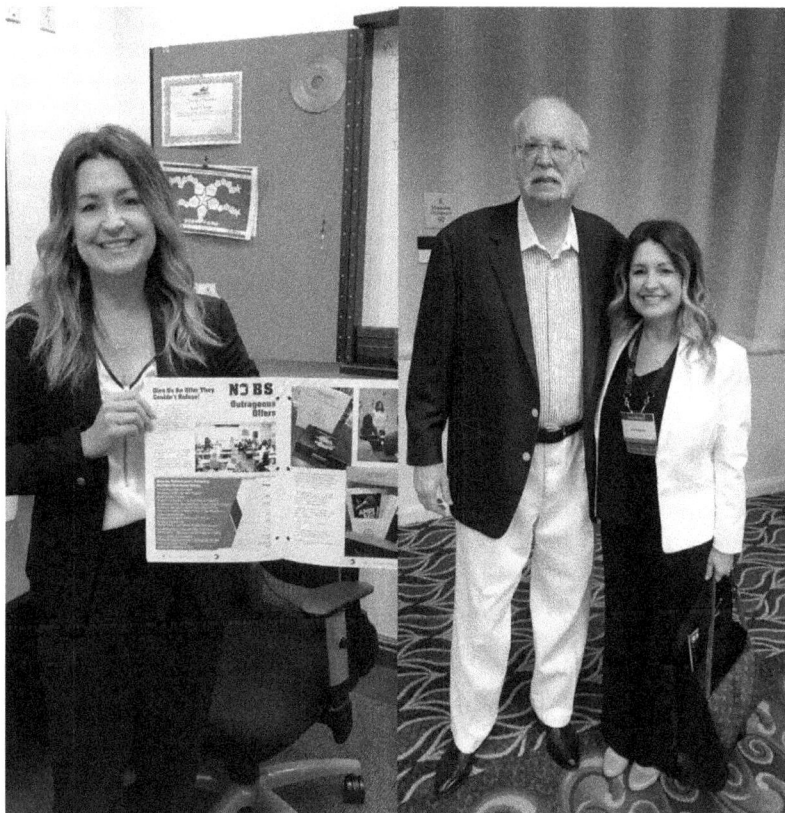

In the summer of 2016 I was asked by a national custom homebuilder to present a series of personal branding workshops to local real estate agents in the state of Florida.

The company, D.R. Horton, needed to strengthen their relationships with realtors in the state and wanted to use workshops and seminars as an opportunity to provide value to the real estate agents and to strengthen their relationships.

When working with the marketing manager for D.R. Horton on a seminar program we decided that a workshop on personal branding would benefit the real estate agents the most. So I presented my signature Claim My Stage personal branding keynote program in three cities for them: Tampa, St. Pete, and Orlando, Florida.

This was an unpaid opportunity but D.R. Horton was very receptive to me making an offer from the stage to compensate me. This way the company would not pay my regular keynote speaking fees saving them thousands of dollars. With their permission I went to work crafting an irresistible offer and a value packed package and program custom for the real estate agents that I knew they would absolutely love.

To design this value-based offer I interviewed many real estate agents that I was either currently working with or was acquainted with and found out that information alone was not enough to help them transform their businesses. They would need support and advice after the event had ended.

So I created a six-week group coaching program that was private to the real estate agents that decided to invest in the program.

In addition to the six-week group coaching program I created a private Facebook group for the agents where they could interact with each other, share best practices, and ask me questions about any issues or roadblocks they came upon.

In addition, I included a copy of my latest book, and tickets to a future live event in the package.

The value of the package was in the thousands of dollars.

When I presented the package to the audience at the end of my presentation, I explained the value of each and every single item that was in the package. I included in the package a blueprint that they could follow to make the most of their investment.

Since real estate agents often work remotely, I included a checklist as well as a guide that could easily fit into their laptop case or handbag so they could refer to it where ever they were.

I thought of all of the different ways I could support them after the sale and built the package around that support so it was custom to them.

The crowd loved it! I was able to sell the package to approximately 25% of the audience members in our three city tour resulting in thousands of dollars in instant sales for my business.

After the event and the sales were complete, of course I focused on delivering an amazing experience and outcomes for each and every real estate agent. They loved the program and left me great reviews. In fact many of them loved the program so much that they ended up just hiring my company to take them to the next level!

I sold the packages to the real estate agents on site only for $297 each. The in-person sales plus additional services purchased after the fact resulted in over tens of thousands of dollars in business for my company.

Many of the real estate agents are still on my email list and in my Facebook group and continue to come to my events, sign up for my programs and purchase my offers.

Because I provided amazing value to the real estate agents and great service after the sale I was able to give them what they wanted and needed to grow their businesses, but I was also able to create a new product that enabled me to grow my business as well.

Results Wrap Up:

If you made the switch to value based pricing and had a process to follow that would empower you to stop competing on price and still provide maximum impact do you think you could be successful?

Yes! You can. To get started, you just need to take the Next Step Action.

Take Action:

1. First, if you are a coach, consultant, or service based provider, remove your prices from your website. This will eliminate price shopping among competitors.
2. Pick one service offering in your business that you want to move away from hourly pricing and move toward value based pricing.
3. Brainstorm and list out all of the various products and services you could include in that new package to give your clients the biggest value and you an amazing payday.

Join the Boss Women Rock community and get access to bonus trainings, resources, and support from amazing people. Join us on Facebook at https:// www.facebook.com/groups/BossWomenRockSuccess

Chapter Six

Direct response conversion and sales tactics to move your followers and fans into paying customers so your marketing isn't just a big waste of time and money.

The goal of this chapter is to convince you that Direct Response marketing is the missing component you need to attract qualified leads, close more sales, and enjoy more profitability in your business.

Gains:

- How to ensure your marketing converts without losing out on missed opportunities to capture a lead or sale
- How to make the switch from brand advertising to direct response marketing without feeling overwhelmed
- How to connect with your prospects and clients at every step in the buyer's journey for maximum results
- How to create content and messaging that gets results

Rumors and Reality:

- You may be thinking that you don't have time to learn a new marketing strategy style, but the truth is direct response marketing will save you time and money.

- You may be thinking that direct response marketing doesn't fit your style, but the truth is if you want to get the most Return on Investment, you will need to adapt and change.

- You may be thinking that direct response marketing is complicated, but the truth is that it is a simple system you can easily follow.

Introduction

Ok, ok… I admit this was not the brightest idea I ever had, but when I was in college, I worked at a bungee jump tourist attraction in Destin, FL one summer.

It was called Air Bongo.

Basically, the idea is that you strap into this harness that's tethered to a 65 foot tower basically made of steel scaffolding by a big elastic cord, and jump off...for fun.

Now, you may be thinking, "Jen, what in the world would you do that for?"

I'll tell you. It was where all the cool kids worked. So, I wanted to do it too.

Yes, my parents literally said, "If all your friends jumped off of a bridge, would you do it too? And I said, "yes."

Stupid. I know.

But, here's what I learned that summer at Air Boingo.

That even scary things can be fun.

That sometimes, we need to break the rules to truly live.

That sometimes, taking a big leap is worth it.

That summer, I built up my bravery muscle. There wasn't anything I was afraid of back then.

I think that's served me well as a business owner and consultant.

As long as you take safety precautions and check your gear, you'll be fine when you take that step off the ledge…

Direct Response marketing is not the type of marketing we are typically exposed to. When we're kids we grow up watching the big brands on TV spending millions on "branding" with commercials that consist of little more than some pretty video, a logo, and a slogan.

But, as small business owners, we can't afford the big brand budgets. Every dollar we spend needs to be trackable, measurable, and get a result.

We can't afford to rely on "branding" alone to make the phone ring.

Usually, our competition is just mimicking what they've seen the big brands do and is wasting money on brand advertising. So, if we do what everyone has always done, we're pretty much guaranteed to fail.

Making the jump from brand advertising to direct response marketing is the single most important jump you will ever make as a business owner.

You can do it, be brave...

Introduction

As consumers of products and services we are most often exposed to a type of marketing which is typically called brand awareness marketing. Brand awareness marketing is adopted by bigger companies like Coca-Cola, Kelloggs, and any company with deep pockets that can afford to spend hundreds of thousands or millions of dollars on TV commercials and other forms of advertising.

These TV commercials typically focus on creating a feel good experience for the viewer and conclude with putting a logo up at the end of the TV spot. Think about the most recent Nike commercial you've seen which probably includes some black and white gritty footage of sweaty athletes with a motivational speech voice over. The commercial fades to black and the Nike swoosh logo pops on screen with "Just Do It." Very rarely do these brand awareness marketing efforts drive a consumers behavior to take immediate action with the company.

As a small business owner we are not afforded the luxury of having hundreds of thousands or millions of dollars and years to spend on brand awareness building.

Every single dollar that we have coming into our business needs to be accounted for, especially in our marketing.

Direct response marketing enables you to get your message in front of the right people, at the right time, and has a focus on measuring results. A mistake I see a lot of experts and influencers making is that they are focused on brand awareness marketing and not on direct response marketing.

The basic idea of direct response marketing is that it will be <u>direct</u> to the ideal perfect client and a <u>response</u> will be measured.

As a keynote speaker at women's business leadership conferences and events, I realize that speaking at events is just the beginning of my relationship with the audience. I need a way to be able to continue the conversation after the show or performance. This is important not only to provide support to the audience members so they can actually implement the ideas that I share with them but also to continue to build my business on the backend.

Sometimes as a speaker I am invited to speak on stages where the event organizers do not pay the speakers. In these cases, it is even more important that I have the ability to monetize that experience after the fact. By focusing on conversions at the event and after the event, I am able to maximize the results for the audience members as well as for my own business.

As you become more highly visible in your career and industry and are asked to speak on podcasts at events or are interviewed in the media, it is important for you to consider how you are going to convert that listener or audience member into a potential prospect or client for you. What is the next step that you want them to take after they see or hear you?

Think of your public appearance as the very first step in the relationship and consider how you want to move that relationship forward.

One idea for how to move an audience member or a listener further along your sales process is to invite them to become a part of your community. Perhaps you have a Facebook group that you could invite the audience members to join.

Another idea to improve conversions is for you to have a free downloadable gift on your website that visitors could access in exchange for their email address.

Perhaps you create a podcast that you could invite them to listen to and subscribe.

As an expert you will be asked to speak on other peoples platforms quite often and you will need to have a plan in place and a systemized process for moving those that connect with you off of other peoples stages and into your own audience and circle of influence.

The golden rule of direct response marketing is that there must always be an offer. An offer doesn't mean that you need to sell. A smarter way to look at district response marketing is to think of it like you are marketing information.

Depending on the type of business that you have you will want to consider one of two strategies: information marketing or information first marketing.

Information Marketing

With information marketing you are marketing your ideas, insights, tools, resources, and anything that is helpful and of use to your viewer, listener, or audience member.

Information marketing is typically used by online marketers who get paid for what they know. Perhaps you are a life coach and have created a course or training on how to thrive during divorce or another unexpected life transition. Maybe you have a membership site where you have stored all of your best ideas and you sell access to the membership site to small business owners as a way for them to self educate. Perhaps you are a coach or consultant who gets paid for your specialized knowledge. In all these cases, information marketing is a powerful way to build your influence and impact in order to build your income.

Webinars and live speaking events are my favorite types of information marketing for my business and I highly recommend mastering the perfect webinar or live event presentation. Send me an email at jen@jendevore.com if you'd like more information on how to do that.

Information First Marketing

Examples of information first marketing include writing books, hosting seminars, providing downloads on your website, or creating podcasts in order to build an audience for your business. Information first marketing works great for businesses like a doctors office, lawyers office, realtor, or a service provider who works directly with clients to help them solve their problems. The great thing about information first marketing is that it can be measured. And remember the first rule of direct response marketing is that everything must be measured.

An example of information first marketing could look like this:

Susan is a commercial real estate advisor who is in a very competitive industry in a competitive market. Susan needs a way to differentiate herself from her competition and is tired of cold calling investors and facing rejection. The investors currently see her as "just another sales person" and not a trusted advisor.

Susan has been listening to podcasts every morning on her run and one day has the epiphany that these real estate advisors on these shows don't know anything more than she does, in fact, she knows deep down inside that she has insights and ideas that could really make a difference if investors just knew the truth.

Taking her frustration from being rejected over and over and seeing a gap in the podcast space for fresh ideas, Susan decides to start a podcast.

On day one, Susan writes a short email and sends it to wealthy investors asking them to be a guest on her podcast show to share how they've been able to become successful in multi-family property investments.

Soon, an amazing thing starts to happen! The commercial real estate investors who typically would not give Susan the time of day are flattered at the opportunity to be interviewed on a show! Let's face it, people love talking about themselves and if you give them a platform they will think that you are influential and powerful and can help them.

So Susan, who has been trying to cold call and cold email these commercial real estate investors has just launched a podcast and now has a foot-in-the-door strategy that's almost guaranteed to work.

With a simple two sentence email she can reach out to other commercial real estate investors and ask them if they like to be a guest on her show. Once they agree she now has a personal relationship with them that puts her on a more even playing field.

The interview is scheduled quite easily by sending a link to an online calendar like Acuity, Schedule Once or Calendly. On the day of the interview Susan sets up a Zoom recorded call to conduct the interview with the commercial real estate investor. The call could be done over video or the call could be done with audio only. Either way it gives Susan the opportunity to connect on a personal and professional level with an investor in a way that few have the ability to do.

From there Susan would take the interview and have it edited by a virtual assistant on a platform like UpWork or Fiverr and then upload the final file to the platform that she hosts the podcast on. The link would be shared with the commercial real estate investor and, you guessed it, the investor would be so proud to be on a podcast that he would share the show link with his other investor friends.

Now that Susan has a compelling foot-in-the-door strategy her work has just begun. She would need to work on converting those investor podcast guests into prospects and then into clients. Susan could develop a VIP email campaign that would go out exclusively to her show guests and continue to provide insights and strategies on the real estate market. She would measure the results of her email marketing campaign and make an offer for a free real estate portfolio review. Her goal is to nurture these prospective clients through time and stay top of mind so that when the investor is ready to buy, she is the go-to-expert they retain.

Most important thing to note: Susan would need to track and measure her results.

Items she could track include:
- Number of podcast interview emails sent each week
- Number of interviews scheduled or yesses received
- Number of subscribers on her list
- Email open rates and click-through rates
- Number of Portfolio Reviews scheduled
- Number of new clients booked

- Number of properties sold
- Value of new business each month, quarter, and year

Are you beginning to see how this could work in your business?

Information marketing is a very powerful way of building bridges and getting your foot in the door where you otherwise might not be able to do it.

Results Wrap Up:

If you had an information marketing campaign powered by direct response that would empower you to maximize every opportunity do you think you could be successful?

Yes! You can. To get started, you just need to take the Next Step Action.

Take Action:

A helpful tool in getting started with direct response marketing is to set up a Daily Operating Control (DOC) board in your office to measure the key units of success for your marketing efforts.

A good place to start with measuring results is with the following:

- Leads - # of calls or contact forms received
- Conversions - # of appointments booked

- Transactions - # of products or services sold
- Price - average dollar sale

If you have a spare whiteboard in your office or are handy with spreadsheets, set up your DOC and start measuring the outcomes in your business on a daily basis.

Join the Boss Women Rock community and get access to bonus trainings, resources, and support from amazing people. Join us on Facebook at https:// www.facebook.com/groups/BossWomenRockSuccess

Chapter Seven

Leveraging small stages and micro-events for maximum income, impact, and influence when the big guys won't let you play in their arenas.

Here's the cold hard truth about speaking in the women in business space: most event organizers don't pay speakers. When I first started on my journey to build an expert business, I focused a lot of energy on trying to get booked as a keynote speaker for women's conferences. I made it my full time job and talked with hundreds of event organizers. I was shocked to find out that in most cases there was NO budget for speakers for events that were built around helping women make money. The irony is not lost on me!

The other issue is that most of the time, the event organizers will not allow speakers to make an offer from the stage. So, how does a professional who speaks leverage events and still make an income?

After that epiphany, I knew I had to pivot my plan. I needed an alternative to speaking on other people's stages. I wanted to host my own events, but I didn't want to break the bank renting out conference spaces. I knew I should start small. Many years later, my small or micro-events are the most profitable strategy in building my coaching business.

For definition purposes, I classify an event as small if it has 16-50 people. I classify it as a micro-event if it has 15 or fewer.

In this chapter, I will share how I leverage small and micro-events for maximum profitability in my business so you can too.

Gains:

- How to host and fill your own small events without spending a dime on marketing or advertising.

- How to ensure participants show up to the event and are engaged even if they've never heard of you before.

- Why micro-events provide the biggest return on investment.

- How to start with the end in mind and design a simple, but effective event flow that converts to new clients every time.

Rumors and Reality:

- You may be thinking that you're not ready to host your own events and prefer to continue networking at other people's events, but the truth is that starting small and hosting your own events doesn't have to be scary and intimidating.

- You may be thinking that hosting events is expensive and requires big advertising budgets, but the truth is that you can fill small and micro-events very easily without spending a dime if you have a solid joint venture partner and an intriguing event focus.

- You may be thinking that hosting events means that it has to be complicated, but if you start small and keep it simple, you can get amazing results.

Introduction

I've been hosting at least two small events or webinars per month for the last two years and it is by far, the #1 one way I grow my business.

The reason why small events work so well, is that our clients are on a journey. It's called the Buyer's Journey. Basically, the Buyer's Journey concept is that people aren't ready to buy from us the first, second, third, fourth, or even fifth time they come into contact with our marketing messages. Like dating, the relationship needs to be built over a process.

Think about it like this: your prospective clients are using the internet to research solutions to their problems. They're gathering information, asking around for reviews, and analyzing their situation. You need to be seen as a trusted advisor and welcome guest in this process and not a pushy, sales-y, unwelcome pest.

Businesses that focus only on making the sale in their marketing, lose out on building trust and more often than not, lose out on many opportunities to capture the 99% of buyers who are not ready to buy from you right now.

Events are a great platform for quickly moving prospective clients down the Buyer's Journey, creating awareness of yourself as an expert, converting them to a prospect by having them attend your event, providing valuable content at the event, making an offer at the event, and closing on the spot. Small events done well, build intimacy, rapport, and develop the know-like-trust factor much faster than traditional sales processes which can take weeks, months, or even years.

In a few hours, over the course of an afternoon, or in the span of a one-hour webinar, you can move prospective clients through most (if not all) of the entire sales process if you have the right people in the room, the right presentation and the right offer.

How to get the right people in the room without spending a dime on advertising.

The foundation of any effective marketing campaign is that it begins with a clearly identified target audience. So, if you want to have effective small or micro-events, you need to have the right messaging for the right people. Saying your business is for "anyone" or casting a wide net to a wide audience is the biggest mistake and will result in a failed campaign or event.

Another big mistake is making your marketing messages more about you and your business and not addressing your prospects pain and frustration. If your marketing messages focus on how many years you've been in business, your credentials, your service offerings, or other self-serving platitudes, you are missing the mark.

Getting the right people in the room means knowing exactly who you work with, what the big (and specific) problem is that they have and you can solve and communicating it in powerful messaging.

To get the right people in the room, I use the little known yet highly effective Conversion Equation.

The Conversion Equation is a simple formula for communicating marketing messages.

The Conversion Equation is comprised of the following:

1. An attention grabbing headline
2. An engaging subheadline that makes the reader want more
3. Both logical and emotional points to prove credibility
4. A compelling offer

The first step in the Conversion Equation is to have an attention grabbing headline that interrupts the reader, listener, or viewer.

How to Write Compelling Headlines:

Here are some examples of attention grabbing headlines:

Life Coach:
"Are you sick and tired of feeling alone and trapped in a loveless marriage?"

Career Coach:

"Does the thought of getting up and going to work on Monday make you want to crawl back in bed?

Business Coach:

"Do you feel frustrated and overwhelmed with marketing and want to throw your computer out the window?

Money Coach:

"Do you avoid opening your bank statements and feel ashamed about how you're managing your household budget?"

Health Coach:

"Are you missing out on precious moments in your life because your health is holding you back?"

Do you see how each headline focuses on a specific pain point or problem that each of the prospects face? The coaches in these marketing examples have clearly addressed what is keeping their ideal prospects up at night and are clearly communicating it in their advertising headline.

The second step in the Conversion Equation is to engage the reader or viewer with a subheadline that makes them want to read more.

How to Write Engaging Sub-Headlines:

Here are some examples of engaging sub-headlines to go with our headlines in the examples above:

Life Coach:

Headline: "Are you sick and tired of feeling alone and trapped in a love-less marriage?"

Subheadline: You're about to discover the one simple concept that could change your relationship forever.

Career Coach:

Headline: "Does the thought of getting up and going to work on Monday make you want to crawl back in bed?

Subheadline: In this inspiring video, you'll hear from people just like you who quit the corporate grind to build success on their terms.

Business Coach:

Headline: "Do you feel frustrated and overwhelmed with marketing and want to throw your computer out the window?

Subheadline: On this live webinar, I'll show you exactly how to generate all the leads you can handle without spending hours trapped behind the computer messing around with Facebook.

Money Coach:

Headline: "Do you avoid opening your bank statements and feel ashamed about how you're managing your household budget?"

Subheadline: At this 2-hour event, we'll explain the one mindset shift you need to make in order to gain back control of your money.

Health Coach:

Headline: "Are you missing out on precious moments in your life because your health is holding you back?"

Subheadline: You're about to find out the truth about what is really preventing you from losing weight and feeling great without going on another fad diet.

Do you see how the subheadline supports the headline and creates an open invitation for the reader, listener or viewer to learn more? We're building curiosity and engaging their imagination.

The next step in the Conversion Equation is to make your case and provide compelling support for your offer on both an emotional logical level.

How to Make Your Case in Marketing Messages:

There are two types of buyers: emotional buyers and logical buyers. Emotional buyers will want to see your testimonials and case studies. Logical buyers will want to see statistics and facts. You will want to have examples of both emotional and logical social proof in your marketing.

Here are some examples of how to make the case for both emotional and logical buyers to go with our headlines and subheadlines in the examples above:

Life Coach:
Headline: "Are you sick and tired of feeling alone and trapped in a loveless marriage?"

Subheadline: You're about to discover the one simple concept that could change your relationship forever.

Social Proof (Logical): 90% of the couples that attend our event leave feeling instantly more connected to their partner.

Social Proof (Emotional): "Attending this event change my life forever. I now know that the secret to a better relationship starts with me." - Susan M., Akron, OH

Career Coach:
Headline: "Does the thought of getting up and going to work on Monday make you want to crawl back in bed?

Subheadline: In this inspiring video, you'll hear from people just like you who quit the corporate grind to build success on their terms.

Social Proof (Logical): 9 out of 10 people who enrolled in our program rated it as "Highly Effective" in helping them transition out of jobs they hated and into careers they love

Social Proof (Emotional): "Before this program, I was so frustrated with my career that it was impacting my marriage. Now I have a job I love and my marriage has never been stronger." Steve G., Austin, TX

Business Coach:

Headline: "Do you feel frustrated and overwhelmed with marketing and want to throw your computer out the window?

Subheadline: On this live webinar, I'll show you exactly how to generate all the leads you can handle without spending hours trapped behind the computer wasting time on social media.

Social Proof (Logical): Out of the 2,341 people that have watched this webinar, over 90% of them say it was the most eye-opening program they've ever seen on how to really grow a business.

Social Proof (Emotional): "Before watching this webinar, I was wasting so much time and money on marketing that my business was about to go bankrupt. Now, I'm making better decisions and my marketing is actually making me money versus costing me money!" Tina S. Denver, CO

Money Coach:

Headline: "Do you avoid opening your bank statements and feel ashamed about how you're managing your household budget?"

Subheadline: At this 2-hour event, we'll explain the one mindset shift you need to make in order to gain back control of your money.

Social Proof (Logical): Event attendees consistently rate this event as "4 out of 5 stars" for time well spent and money saved.

Social Proof (Emotional): "I used to throw my bank statements away without even opening them because I was so fearful of what it would say. But, now I feel in control of my finances and no longer fear the mailbox!" Jonathan, Dallas, TX

Health Coach:
Headline: "Are you missing out on precious moments in your life because your health is holding you back?"

Subheadline: You're about to find out the truth about what is really preventing you from losing weight and feeling great without going on another fad diet.

Social Proof (Logical): The Association of Nutritionists has given their seal of approval for this program.

Social Proof (Emotional): "For years, I struggled with the energy to play with my kids. Now, I can keep up with them and play for hours running on the beach and at the park." Sam, Ft. Lauderdale, FL

Do you see how the Social Proof "makes the case" in the marketing without the business owners having to seem braggadocious or self-serving? We're building a solid case for our offer coming up next.

The final step in the Conversion Equation is to make a compelling offer that is hard to resist. Now, remember that if you're trying to fill small or micro-events, your offer is going to a seat at the table, an admission ticket, or entrance to the webinar, class or program.

Key components of a compelling offer are that it is:

- The appropriate offer for the right step in the Buyer's Journey
- Moves the reader, viewer or listener to take action
- Is clear and concise and not complicated
- Is easy to understand and directional

Here are some examples of how to make an offer that is compelling and moves people to action.

Life Coach:
Headline: "Are you sick and tired of feeling alone and trapped in a loveless marriage?"

Subheadline: You're about to discover the one simple concept that could change your relationship forever.

Social Proof (Logical): 90% of the couples that attend our event leave feeling instantly more connected to their partner.

Social Proof (Emotional): "Attending this event change my life forever. I now know that the secret to a better relationship starts with me." - Susan M., Akron, OH

Offer: Buy One Ticket, Bring Your Spouse for Free. Save your seats at this event by clicking HERE.

Career Coach:
Headline: "Does the thought of getting up and going to work on Monday make you want to crawl back in bed?

Subheadline: In this inspiring video, you'll hear from people just like you who quit the corporate grind to build success on their terms.

Social Proof (Logical): 9 out of 10 people who enrolled in our program rated it as "Highly Effective" in helping them transition out of jobs they hated and into careers they love

Social Proof (Emotional): "Before this program, I was so frustrated with my career that it was impacting my marriage. Now I have a job I love and my marriage has never been stronger." Steve G., Austin, TX

Offer: Click HERE to watch this life changing video on-demand

Business Coach:
Headline: "Do you feel frustrated and overwhelmed with marketing and want to throw your computer out the window?

Subheadline: On this live webinar, I'll show you exactly how to generate all the leads you can handle without spending hours trapped behind the computer wasting time on social media.

Social Proof (Logical): Out of the 2,341 people that have watched this webinar, over 90% of them say it was the most eye-opening program they've ever seen on how to really grow a business.

Social Proof (Emotional): "Before watching this webinar, I was wasting so much time and money on marketing that my business was about to go bankrupt. Now, I'm making better decisions and my marketing is actually making me money versus costing me money!" Tina S. Denver, CO

Offer: Webinar starts in 15 minutes. Click here to register now!

Money Coach:
Headline: "Do you avoid opening your bank statements and feel ashamed about how you're managing your household budget?"

Subheadline: At this 2-hour event, we'll explain the one mindset shift you need to make in order to gain back control of your money.

Social Proof (Logical): Event attendees consistently rate this event as "4 out of 5 stars" for time well spent and money saved.

Social Proof (Emotional): "I used to throw my bank statements away without even opening them because I was so fearful of what it would say. But, now I feel in control of my finances and no longer fear the mailbox!" Jonathan, Dallas, TX

Offer: End Money Fear Forever! Click here to save your seat.

Health Coach:
Headline: "Are you missing out on precious moments in your life because your health is holding you back?"

Subheadline: You're about to find out the truth about what is really preventing you from losing weight and feeling great without going on another fad diet.

Social Proof (Logical): The Association of Nutritionists has given their seal of approval for this program.

Social Proof (Emotional): "For years, I struggled with the energy to play with my kids. Now, I can keep up with them and play for hours running on the beach and at the park." Sam, Ft. Lauderdale, FL

Offer: Click here to download the eBook that could change the way you look at food forever and get a free ticket to an upcoming event.

Without spending an additional dime on marketing, these coaches could drastically improve the results of their marketing and fill rooms and programs with ease.

The examples of compelling copy I provided above are not meant to be complete sales pages or advertising examples. They are meant to show you the step by step process to creating compelling copy that moves people to action. Creating compelling copy is process and takes time. Your sales pages, invitations, and ads may have more or less copy that what I've shown as an example.

To download a copy of the Conversion Equation worksheet you can use to grade your copywriting skills, please visit the Files section of the Boss Women Rock Rockstar Results Academy Facebook Group.

Join the Boss Women Rock community and get access to bonus trainings, resources, and support from amazing people. Join us on Facebook at https:// www.facebook.com/groups/BossWomenRockSuccess

How to craft the perfect presentation so you can rest assured that your event will convert prospects to clients.

Have you ever been in a presentation or speech where the presenter was clearly clueless about what the audience needed to hear or what problem they were there to solve?

Have you ever seen a presenter ramble on and on through a Power-point slide deck that was filled with self-serving platitudes, company history, boring facts and details about their products and services leaving the audience members feeling bored, annoyed, and cheated?

Have you ever personally worked very hard on a presentation, received great reviews only to have it flop when it came time to monetizing?

A major key to building a successful coaching, consulting, or service based business is that you must have a signature presentation that both provides massive value to the audience AND can convert them to prospects or buyers.

The reason why you want to have a signature presentation is that it can be very time consuming to create new slide decks and come up with new content time after time. If your message is constantly changing, it will be hard to become known as the go-to expert in your field. Also, you won't be able to know why some of your presentations go great and others miss the mark if you're constantly changing it.

Usually the thing that keeps us from honing in on a signature presentation is that we bend our message to meet markets that aren't ideal for us. When you stay true to who you serve and stay on message, you can be much more impactful.

You don't need to recreate the wheel every time you speak. Think about it this way: Broadway performers don't change their show every night, so why should you? They focus on creating and performing ONE show at an expert level and deliver the same lines over and over. Now, their performance may change night to night, but since they are working and developing the ONE show, they are able to precisely perfect each moment in the performance and deliver great results with confidence.

In order to create your ONE signature presentation, my best advice is to use the template, outline, and flow created by the master Russell Brunson of ClickFunnels.

Before I found Russell's "Perfect Webinar" script, my former business partners and I invested about 3 years and $20,000 in training with Speaking Empire to create a signature talk. Now, I'm not saying that the training wasn't valuable. It was! But, I could have saved myself tons of time and money if I would have known about Russells' format beforehand.

Russell is a student of Dan Kennedy who is the direct response market-er that I have studied for years as well. The industry calls Dan Kennedy "The Millionaire Maker." Russell has broken down the "Perfect Webi-nar" or as I call it the "Perfect Presentation" into a simple and easy to follow format that you can use to quickly and easily make a presenta-tion that will convert and result in sales.

If you don't follow Russell, he is the world's best expert at converting with presentations with results that are truly mind blowing. In fact, he recently made $3 million dollars in 90 minutes using the exact formula he shares with us at the Grant Cardone 10X event.

I personally have used his exact process to convert 20-25% of an audi-ence into paid clients consistently for years.

Let's do the simple math so you can see why this formula could be so powerful:

- Let's say (hypothetically) that you speak at an event or have a webinar that has 30 people (of your ideal prospects) in attendance.
- Using Russell's template and training, you deliver your signature presentation and convert 20% of the room into paying clients.
- You could have 6 new clients.
- If your offer is $297 you could make $1,782 in 90 minutes or less.

- If your offer is $1,000 you could make $6,000 in 90 minutes or less.

- If you offer is $3,000 you could make $18,000 in 90 minutes or less.

- If your offer is $10,000 you could make $60,000 in 90 minutes or less.

After I created the first draft of my signature presentation using Russell's format, I started out slow with making offers around $297. Once I mastered that level and increased my confidence, I now personally and consistently convert 20% of the room at the $1,000 level with ease. It's now time for me to level up my game and increase the price of my offer.

Now, you might be thinking:

"But... I sell things offline..."

"But... I'm in the eCommerce space..."

"But... I have a service-based business..."

No more "buts" about it!

We have proven over the last 10 years that the Perfect Webinar blueprint literally sells anything and everything.

If you're selling eCommerce products this will work for you...

Many of our eCommerce sellers who have mastered the Perfect Webinar will bundle a bunch of their products together, make a kit, sell it on the webinar and make more money in a day than they typically make in an entire month.

Professional services?...

Do a webinar... at the end pitch people your services and you'll get clients at higher fees with a lot less drama...

Network Marketers:

The Perfect Webinar to date has helped people in your industry make well over $100 million (and that's just what we can track...)

The Perfect Webinar works... it's perfect... don't screw it up... don't deviate from it.

You can plug any product or service you want into this blueprint and it will sell it for you...

Don't believe me?...

Give it a try...

Claim Your Perfect Webinar Script Here >> https://jendevore.com/training

But be sure not to mess it up!

The only time I've seen it not work is when people don't follow the script the right way...

Every one of those pieces we put in there is from what my friend Russell learned in his 10 year journey of speaking on stage after stage after stage...

10 years of presenting and failing... bruising hsi knees and bloodying his knuckles testing everything in front of live audiences until we knew exactly what worked and what didn't work...

Some things might not make much sense at first... but trust me, they work!

It's kind of like Mr. Miyagi in Karate Kid...

Mr. Miyagi tells to paint the fence and wax the car...

At first Daniel doesn't understand...

He approaches Mr. Miyagi later in frustration and tells him, "I quit! I'm not here to do your chores... I'm here to do Karate..."

Then Mr. Miyagi throws a punch at Daniel and he instinctively waxes the car and blocks his punch...

At that moment Daniel knew why Mr. Miyagi was having him do these weird things.

The same thing will happen to you when you do your first Perfect Webinar and follow the script and your sales start coming in...

You'll feel your heart beating faster and faster when you realize that this is it... this is the key to your future...

That's what I want you to understand.

So even though some parts don't make sense right now... trust me, they work.

"Wax the car" and "paint the fence" with me for a little bit and prove me wrong... :)

Worst case scenario, you're right...

Best case scenario, you make a whole bunch of money...

So go get a copy of the Perfect Webinar Script here:

Claim Your Perfect Webinar Script Here >> https://jendevore.com/training

I am 100% positive that this will be a powerful tool to growing your conversion rate and closing more sales.

How to make an offer at the end of your presentation without feeling slimy or salesy.

One of the most commonly asked questions I get is "how do you sell without being sales-y or slimy?"

First, I think it's important for us to reframe our brain around what it means to sell. To me, selling is making the world a better place by offering a solution to a problem.

If you're selling something like coaching, consulting, or a service that truly has the ability to change someone's life forever, where is the harm in that?

If you can improve someone's life, marriage, career, money situation, relationships, or family forever, you owe it to them to make an offer. Not making an offer is actually the worst thing you can do to them.

Selling gets a bad rap because of old stereotypes we have about underhanded sales people pushing products and services on us that we didn't really need or want just because the were trying to make a sales quota or goal.

But, we as professionals in servitude, don't have to worry about that because we are only offering real solutions to real problems. We're connecting with the right audience and we're developing our programs to be transformational and outcomes based. We're coming from a place of love and not of greed.

That said, there are a few key concepts that I have implemented that help me close more business without being pushy.

1. Implement an application process up front
2. Demonstrate value during the sales process
3. Ask permission to present a solution
4. Let the client determine the next step

Implement an application process up front

Has a prospective client ever told you, "all you consultants are all the same" and when they said it they didn't mean it in a nice way.

Sometimes, there are members of our profession that give the industry a bad rap. Perhaps they over promise and under deliver, perhaps they sell without the clients best interest at heart, perhaps they disappear after the sale and don't stay connected leaving the client feeling high and dry.

As experts, we need to separate ourselves from the negative connotations that may be attached to our professions.

One way to do that is to do the exact opposite of what our competition is doing in the sales process.

While others will take any client that comes along even if it's not the right fit because they need the money, we will implement a match-making process in our business by having the client apply to work with us.

Before I started implementing an application process for clients, I wasted hours and hours dealing with tire kickers, price shoppers, time wasters, and idea stealers.

After implementing an application process, I cut out wasted time on calls with people that are not the best fit for me. It shows them that I'm serious about working with the right people and committed to only working with those that I know I can get a great result for in my programs.

The application also makes it seem as though your time is valuable (because it is) and puts scarcity on your availability. Scarcity is a powerful motivator in sales.

So, at the end of each one of my presentations, I invite the participants to apply to work with me by giving them a link to my calendar which automatically sends them the application to fill out before our call.

The two tools I use to accomplish that easily and automatically are Calendly and an application I built in ClickFunnels. You could just use Google Forms if you don't have ClickFunnels.

Demonstrate value during the sales process

Once the prospective client has scheduled their call with me and filled out their application, I focus on making that 45 minute call the best 45 minutes they will spend all week working on their business.

I don't make the sales process all about me. I make it about them!

There's this little-known thing called Profit Hacking. Hardly anybody is talking about it. But when you learn it and use it, you'll see a huge difference in your small business marketing and immediately understand how fast you can make an extra $10K next quarter by uncovering hidden revenue opportunities in your business.

According to Shark Tank's Kevin O'Leary, women entrepreneurs are "100% of the time his best investment" because we are excellent at time management, we set realistic goals, our company cultures have less turnover, we take feedback and implement it, and we have consistency in our brands.

The problem is that women are overwhelmed and frustrated by the bad information from so-called marketing gurus on how to grow a business. They jump from shiny object to shiny object and get lackluster outcomes resulting in an 80% failure rate in the first 18 months. The existing entrepreneurial education system lacks a simple process that tells the truth about what it really takes to succeed.

Kevin O'Leary from Shark Tank says that "knowing your numbers, profitability potential, and your ability to sell your concept and self" are the key factors to entrepreneurial success, yet women just do not know these 3 important concepts.

These concepts are not taught in schools, unless you have an MBA, and the traditional women's networking groups focus on "soft topic" concepts like confidence and work-life balance instead of the hard-hitting facts about business growth.

My sales process is unlike any other in that we are the only system that uses Direct Response Marketing principles to uncover Profitability Potential for each one of our members individually.

My unique promise (or Market Dominating Position) is that I can uncover $50,000 - $100,000 in hidden revenue in 45 minutes or less, guaranteed.

On average, I find about $44,500 to $314,000 in low hanging fruit hidden revenue opportunities for each person I do a 45-minute call with. Now THAT is providing massive value during the sales process.

If you'd like to schedule a call with me for your business, apply at: https://calendly.com/jenrichter/business-breakthrough

Ask permission to present a solution

As I near the end of my 45 minute business breakthrough call, the listener is usually on the edge of their seat with excitement about the profit potential in their business. Once I start to uncover the opportunity, the next step is simply if they want me to help them implement the concepts or not.

So, my two favorite phrases for closing more sales without feeling sales-y are:

"Would you like me to help you implement that?

Or

"Where do you think we should go from here?"

Notice how I don't automatically go into pitching my services. It's important to ask permission to present solutions and services. This way you are seen as a welcome guest and not an unwelcome pest.

If I'm conducting a presentation on stage or in a webinar, I simply use the phrase:

"Do you see yourself doing this?

And

"Would it be ok if I showed you my system for getting results?

It's amazing at how disarming those simple questions can be paving the way for a much smoother sales process for both you and the prospective client.

Let the client determine the next step

Now that you have received permission to present solutions, the final concept is to give your client your recommendation based on their exact situation and let them determine if that is the right step for them.

Just like a medical doctor prescribes a treatment plan for what ails a patient, we too can prescribe solutions to our clients.

Don't make it complicated or hard to buy from you.

By limiting the options and making a professional recommendation, you empower the potential client because they are armed with the information they need to make a good decision.

It is important that you have two things along with your recommendation: an upsell and a downsell.

Did you know that 34% of buyers will upgrade to the bigger package when you offer it to them? If you don't have a Premium package, create one as soon as possible so you have a powerful and profitable upsell.

But, what if the solution you present doesn't fit in the client budget? Then you will need to have a downsell. A downsell is when the client declines your package, but you offer them an alternative solution at a lower price.

By having ONE recommended solution, plus an upsell and downsell packages, you will be able to hit the "sweet spot" in your pricing and empower your client to make the best decision for them.

Results Wrap Up:

I hope you see now that you can be successful speaking at events and on webinars by having a proven sales process for both presentation and the offer. It's all in how it's positioned.

To get started building your business through speaking and event, you just need to take the Next Step Action.

Take Action:

- Claim Your Perfect Webinar Script Here >>https://jendevore. com/training

Join the Boss Women Rock community and get access to bonus trainings, resources, and support from amazing people. Join us on Facebook at https:// www.facebook.com/groups/BossWomenRockSuccess

After Word

Jen here from Boss Women Rock with a quick story for you.

A lot of people have asked why I created Boss Women Rock... what's the story behind all this hard work and dedication?

Of course, we're all about helping you get great results with your expert business. That's our #1 goal!

But our commitment and dedication to help you build your business without wasting time and money goes deeper than that... much deeper!

So we wanted to share with you the story behind Boss Women Rock so you can understand the reason we do what we do and why we care so much about your expert business success.

I have been working with business owners now for years and I have seen first hand all of the problems and heard all of the bad information in the "women's empowerment" space and I can't stand by and let it continue any longer.

The same bad information being shared. The same focus on everything else but RESULTS.

Gurus sharing the latest tip, trick, or tactic but not sharing the behind-the-scenes TRUTH about what is really needed to grow a business.

Business owners who are confused and overwhelmed.

80% of them going OUT OF BUSINESS in 18 months.

50% of the rest OUT OF BUSINESS in the first 5 years.

The technology constantly changing making marketing costly and cumbersome.

Women pouring their heart and soul into their business, running from networking event to networking event trying to chase down the next lead.

Me wishing that SOMEONE would step up and yell ENOUGH!

No one ever did.

Gurus kept selling courses and hid behind their computers. Good luck trying to get one to answer a simple question!

Groups kept on taking people's money and members struggled to scale their businesses.

Consultants selling tactics and projects, but not strategy and solid advice.

So I decided to fix the problems.

Boss Women Rock is a movement for those that are serious about their business in the coaching, consulting, or service based industries of health, wealth, or relationships.

Who is it for? Influencers, changemakers, light spreaders, and truth seekers.

Boss Women Rock is NOT just another program or course.

We are not just dumping more information on you.

Need to ask a question about how to generate leads and need a REAL, LIVE response from a proven expert?

Need to get an example of a landing page, an ad, or a sales letter so you don't have to recreate

the wheel and hire an expensive agency?

Need to get some training on how to close more sales, but don't want to drop thousands on another "motivational" conference?

Want to connect with other professionals from across the globe?

Want special discounts on training events, recommended courses and software tools? Some of them FREE!

Want access to the exclusive printed magazine (shipped to your door), phone call Q&As and tutorials for Boss Women Rock members only? OF COURSE YOU DO!

We offer all of this in one package for one small monthly fee. EVERY-THING is included. This small fee is no different than a business collecting a cover charge. This ensures that only those women serious about their business join.

The quality of the content and the other Boss Women will truly take your business to the next level.

So, that's the story behind Boss Women Rock.

And as you can see, what we do and why we care about you and your results goes way deeper than just "expert business."

I invite you to check us out in our Public Facebook group at:

https://www.facebook.com/groups/BossWomenRockSuccess/

To your success!

Jen DeVore Richter
CEO & Founder
Boss Women Rock™

PS - We want to hear YOUR story about how Boss Women Rock changes your life when it comes to building your expert business :-) Connect with us on Facebook right now!

In 2017, I landed $108,000 in free publicity and used the attention to build my credibility faster so I could focus on claiming her own stage. In industry circles, I am known as the Powerhouse Producer of Rising Influencers™. I help my clients earn more by focusing on just 5 key areas of their business.

Now, I am sharing my proven process for maximizing profitability in any business. I call it the Rising Influencer Profit Process™.

Free Offer from Jen DeVore Richter

Attract Your Ideal Perfect, People With Ease With My Proven Formula

FREE GIFT

Video Training Series

Downloadable Worksheets Included

Claim your $433.61 worth of pure, money magnet, business building strategies that work ABSOLUTELY FREE.

All you have to do is go here now:

www.jendevore.com/people-magnet

www.ingramcontent.com/pod-product-compliance
Lightning Source LLC
Chambersburg PA
CBHW072313210326
41519CB00057B/4903